Winged with Longing for Better Things

SYLVIA SWEENEY
Poetry by Kimlee Anslow Hayes

CHURCH
PUBLISHING
INCORPORATED

Scripture passages in this book are the author's adaptations based
on the New Revised Standard Version.

Church Publishing
19 East 34th Street
New York, NY 10016
www.churchpublishing.org

Cover design, interior design, and typesetting by Beth Oberholtzer

ISBN-13: 978-1-64065-142-5 (pbk.)
ISBN-13: 978-1-64065-143-2 (ebook)

CONTENTS

AUTHOR'S NOTE

There is a Celtic phrase, *anam cara*, for a spiritual friend who journeys through life with us, offering wisdom, love, and encouragement as we wander the spiritual road from childhood innocence to our last days. For over forty years I have had such a friend. She is a wonderful poet, and when I began this book, I asked her if she might allow me to print some of her poems in this Lenten devotional to add another layer of depth and wisdom to what I wrote and the photograph I took. Kimlee Anslow Hayes has offered a poem for each day of Lent to accompany the scriptures I've chosen and the meditations and prayers I've written. On first blush one may wonder, "Why this poem in this place?" I find that each poem does make a connection to what preceded it, and I hope you will find as much blessing and delight in finding some connection as I have. I want to offer special thanks to Kim for making this book so much more than it could have been otherwise.

I also want to thank the Board of Trustees of Bloy House, the Episcopal Theological School at Claremont for the sabbatical that made this book possible, the Conant Fund of the Episcopal Church for the sabbatical grant that allowed me to travel to all the places described in the book, Bob Honeychurch, who traveled those thousands of miles as my companion and chauffeur, and Molly Sweeney for all her editorial support during the writing process.

INTRODUCTION

This is not your typical Lenten devotional. It grows out of years of research about the history of Ash Wednesday and Lent and some persistent intuitions about what is being asked of Christians in the twenty-first century. Many have noted that perhaps the best corollary we will find to Christian life in our day is that of life in the early centuries of the church before Christendom developed. This was a world in which knowledge of the practices, tenets, and spirituality of Christians was not widely known, when the world beyond the doors of the church—which was understood to be much more a people gathered than a place to gather—was ruled by forces unsympathetic to Christian life and Christian ethics.

In this world, to become a Christian meant first becoming acquainted with a Christian who could show one the way. Friends, neighbors, shopkeepers, and relatives could serve as the conduit for faith, modeling a life different from much of the pessimism, isolationism, classism, and consumerism expressed by the crumbling society of the late Roman Empire. If the elements of Christian life came to be deeply attractive—as they did for many in the first through early fourth centuries, then a spiritual seeker might begin to make inquiries about the faith. That would lead to a more intentional process of evangelization. Sharing the gift of faith was the honor and privilege of every Christian. To be sought out as a godparent for a potential adult convert to the faith was a sign and symbol of all that it meant to be a Christ bearer.

While practices varied across the centuries and geography of the Christian diaspora, there are written testimonies to certain practices that perhaps have the greatest potential for helping us to shape the nature of individual and corporate Christian life now. One important element to life in this age was the importance of each baptized person.

The church has always had leaders. The power and privilege held by those leaders has been shaped and reshaped over millennia by the ways in which power was understood within the church and within the society. Leadership in the first three centuries of the church was often less formal in tone and in character. Leaders were formed out of their experiences of faith and their visible charisms for caring for the members of the body of Christ. While leaders were seen as representatives of Christ to the world, so were all baptized persons. Leaders were simply those within a given Christian community whose gifts for teaching, nurturing, and administration made them the natural choices for those positions. In time, these leaders came to be called bishops, bishops who were surrounded by presbyters, elder members of the community who offered them support and counsel. Effective administration of the human and economic resources of a community often took place through the efforts of deacons. In its beginnings, leadership within the Christian community was ideally less about power and more about service to the greater good.

In this setting the source of power was spiritual rather than political. It was the demonstration of the charisms of the Spirit that led to one's designation as a leader. It was the Spirit that held the power, not the leader. And the Spirit resided not in any one person, but in all baptized persons and most profoundly and full-throatedly in the gathered assembly. Christians were individuals whose lives had been transformed by the Spirit working in and through a holy community.

By definition, to be a Christian meant to live one's life in such a way that one became a light to the world, calling others out of their lostness into new life and new hope. To be a Christian meant that one had already thrown off the chains of this world and made a conscious choice to live as Christ lived. To be a Christian meant that at least twice a day one renewed one's commitment to sanctity through stopping to pray the prayer that Christ taught us. To be a Christian also meant gathering with other Christians for the breaking of bread and the offering of prayers of intercession and thanksgiving to God.

The Christian life was meant to be lived in holy community with other holy people. It would be in the sharing, the learning, the mutual caretaking of life lived together, that one would continue to grow deeper into the stature of Christ. Day by day by day. Learning. Growing. Allowing the Spirit to intercede for them in ways they could not always recognize or understand. Sanctity was not the work of a season: it was the work of each day, leading to a lifetime of transformation, renewal, and healing.

In the second and third centuries the processes by which one experienced conversion to the faith, to this communal sanctified life, and received baptism came to be more formalized in some settings. While individual godparents continued to be the touchstone to Christianity and central figures in the earliest stages of evangelization, the church also came to see the value of offering periods of intense formalized learning and preparation for those to be baptized, now called catechumens. Easter came to be the natural choice for baptism, the annual commemoration of Jesus's resurrection and humanity's salvation. Just as Jesus spent forty days in the wilderness prior to beginning his ministry, those preparing to be baptized were invited into a forty-day period of preparation. At the same time, the whole church entered into this season of preparation for their great feast day, and one of the most important aspects was walking alongside those who were about to be baptized. It was in this action of solidarity and advocacy that one could most fully remember and most deeply embrace that gracious God-given moment of being made a Christ bearer—one in whom the Spirit of Christ lived and dwelt.

Praying, interceding, advocating on behalf of these courageous catechumens became the demanding work of the church during the season of Lent. One prepared for Easter by walking alongside, learning alongside, and praying for those who—at least in some settings—were not yet considered holy enough to participate even in the prayers of the faithful. It was through baptism that one was washed and reborn and made ready to receive the blessed food and drink of unending life (the Eucharist) and to participate in the holy prayers of the faithful. One dare never forget the extraordinary graciousness of that baptism, that moment of surrender and acceptance by God and the church. To relive it through witnessing, praying for, and supporting the conversion of new converts was to keep alive in oneself the profundity of the gift of salvation.

From the time of the first Roman persecutions on into the second, third, and fourth centuries, another phenomenon developed. Those who had recanted their faith in times of persecution and peril became cut off from the church. They were shunned informally in the beginning for renouncing their faith and then through excommunication as the church became more formal in its structures and roles. Easter also offered the opportunity for these notorious sinners who had begged God and the church for forgiveness to be returned to the faith and welcomed back into community. This too, like the catechumenate, evolved into ritualized processes that involved confessions, exorcisms, teaching, and acts of charity and compassion. This process of re-sanctification was seen to be possible as a result of the prayers and intercessions of the faithful on behalf of those who had lost their faith. Lent became, in addition to the preparation of catechumens, a period of preparation to receive members of the order of penitents back into the fold. For both groups penitential practices were a critical element of their process of conversion or reconversion. By confessing, by showing penitence, by making amends, by changing one's life, by learning the faith, by living in charity, and by fervent prayer one prepared for Easter; and the church in absolute solidarity prepared alongside.

As the church moved deeper into the fourth, fifth, sixth, and early medieval centuries, Christendom took hold when Christianity became the religion of the empire. The overwhelming majority of the inhabitants of the now Holy Roman Empire were Christians, having been baptized as infants as members of a believing household. The catechumenate as it had formerly existed dissolved. The order of penitents also dissolved as Christianity's identity as a holy people diluted within the mix and mingle of normal everyday life in the empire. In response to this loss of sanctity and devaluation of the holiness of the baptized, Lent took a turn.

When there were no longer catechumens to advocate for or penitents to stand alongside, the church in its desire to maintain the sanctity of the Feast of the Resurrection reshaped its understanding of Lent to assert that it was not the Christian's holiness that was the impetus for Lenten disciplines. It was the Christian's sinfulness. When the order of penitents ceased to exist, the church's response was to transform the identity of the church from the holy people of God to the sin-sick people of God. Instead of advocating and interceding for others, the work of Lent became the work of contrition and petition for oneself. The locus of Christian life moved in many ways from "we" to "me."

It is this focus on "me" that has framed much of our Lenten discipline for the last 1600 years. Christians have come to see Lent as being about our own salvation and our need for reparation and restitution and sanctification; we seem to have forgotten that we have been called to be advocates and intercessors for a world in need of Christ's transformative healing power. We have been so busy trying to find healing for ourselves that we have often forgotten that our healing has already come. It is the world full of suffering around us that begs to be healed.

Many of us in the West no longer live in a world where Christendom exists: where the vast majority of citizens of a nation claim Christianity as their religion and engage in its practices. In much of the world this was never the case. For the most part, in this century those who are Christians are Christians by choice, not by circumstance. To attend church, to offer prayers, to model one's life after Jesus, to engage in spiritual disciplines that form one more fully into the image of Christ: these are actions undertaken by most Christians. Most often, they are actions that are neither understood or supported by the political, social, and economic structures of our day. Christians are becoming once again a people set apart; a people who have responded to God's gracious invitation to a holy life. This holy life is, according to the central tenets of the Christian faith, a life that is spent loving one's neighbor as oneself.

What might Lent look like if we spent those forty days actively seeking to love our neighbors as ourselves with a renewed level of intentionality and focus? What neighbors might we most need to shower our love upon? Who might God be asking us to advocate and intercede for in this fast-paced, technologically and economically driven day? Do we have a love of self that allows us to reach out to the world in this way, or is that also part of the learning we must do?

With every day's news, we know that the breadth of need for our prayers is greater than we have ever before recognized. If the early church was especially focused on the needs of the poor, the marginalized, and those in need of help and healing, the same must be said of us. Only now, the poor, the marginalized, and those in need of help and healing include not only legions of humans living in the midst of poverty and oppression, but also an entire planet suffering at the hands of a powerful and self-aggrandizing few. Contemporary Western Christians are very often both the advocate and the penitent simultaneously. We are the oppressors. We are the oppressed. We are the perpetrators of environmental disaster and will be its victims. We can also be the Spirit-led advocates for those who find themselves most oppressed, living life at calamity's edge.

This Lenten resource is designed to both give us pause and to call us to prayer and action. It is an invitation to focus less on our individual sin or even our corporate sin, but instead to move from the role of penitent to that of advocate. For centuries we have told God how sorry we are. It is not enough to be sorry. If one wants to claim one's own faith, one must move from penitence to sanctification; from believing in our own sinfulness to believing in our own potential for God-given holiness. This book is a call to believe in our own goodness even as we continue to look courageously at our own corporate choices and actions, the source of endless suffering in our world.

This book is also an invitation to an eco-feminist perspective. As an ecofeminist, I look at life's questions through the lens of a woman, a woman who is part of a much larger ecology, seeking to understand the many dimensions of the biological, social, political, and spiritual environment in which I live. For me, the solutions to life's problems can only be found when those problems are viewed from the perspective of every manner and condition of men, and women, and children, and all God's creatures, animate and inanimate.

Eco-feminism actively embraces the physicality of our created identity. We are bodies. We are meant to experience life and God through those bodies. We are invited by God to embrace our own bodiliness, not deny it. While portions of ancient Greek philosophy may have denigrated and rejected the body, that is not an appropriate response for a faith community that believes in the goodness of creation as presented in Genesis or the gift of the incarnation as presented in the gospels. All of God's creatures are created bodies and all are equally loved, valued, and cherished by the creator. To deny this truth is to stand against the very character of God's relationship to God's beloved world. The life we live, the vision we would build for the world, must fit within this framework of created goodness and belovedness.

Whenever we build our world *as if*—as if only some matter and not all; as if only men lived here and not women; as if the world were created exclusively for human beings and their needs; as if it were possible to make some portion of God's created world invisible so that we can find simpler answers to our own individual challenges—we harm the very fabric of human life. It is only in our wholeness, our physicality, our bodiliness, our creatureliness that we can truly hear God's Spirit most fully and completely. It is in our embodied consciousness that we can embrace the mission God has given the church. It is our mission and our challenge as Christians to be advocates for all those creatures of God who are at risk of being abused, ignored, dismissed, or forgotten. That includes most of the world's women and girls. Consider someone you feel is at risk of being abused, ignored, forgotten, or discounted by our church or our society. If you were to see yourself as an advocate for them, what would you want to advocate for?

Sometimes Christians forget that in the early church the period of the forty days of Lent was not so much about penitence as it was about intercession and advocacy for those who were penitents. It was the work of the church to nurture, to intercede for, and to advocate for those catechumens and individuals in the penitential order who hoped to be welcomed into the community of faith at Easter. The church's prayers and soul searching were done as a form of solidarity with those about to enter or re-enter the church. Interceding, mentoring, sharing, and being a companion was the work of the church during the time immediately before Easter. Advocacy work lies at the heart of the Christian life. We are made Christians so that we can share salvation with others along the way. Not so we can hold it for ourselves. In the early church perfection was not to be found in some private interior world so much as in learning how to live in and express God's perfect love to the world and for the world.

How might our church and our world be changed if taking on the role of companion and advocate were a part of our core mission? How might the ministries already coming to fruition through the work of our communities become more visible (or at least less invisible) and more listened to if advocacy became central to our purposes? In what ways has the part of the body of Christ you participate in already begun to commit itself to that work?

Because life is lived most fully in the particular, rather than in the theoretical, I have shaped the reflections that follow around a set of geographic particularities that grow out of my own life experience. For each of the weeks of Lent, this book will present the story of a place in the Intermountain West of the United States. The Intermountain West contains some of the most majestic and awe-inspiring landscapes on planet Earth. The same forces that created that profound beauty also left behind vast riches of natural resources, resources that for several hundred years have now been plundered in ways that one can only describe as selfish, profane, obscene, and ethically unconscionable. As we spend this season of Lent interceding for those most in need of God's help—including interceding by using our hands to bring about that help, let us remember. Let us remember a land and a people, knowing that the stories being told about this place and its peoples can also be told about vast swaths of this planet from the Antarctic to the rainforests of South America to the disappearing islands of the Pacific to the various cultural and geographic regions of North America.

May you find through this book a pathway into your own holiness, the goodness that resides within you. May you be emboldened to think, to speak, to pray, to act, and to dream of a world as Clement wrote in the first century, "winged with longing for better things."

Libby, Montana

LIZZY LIVED IN THE TINY LOGGING TOWN of Libby in northwest Montana. She'd grown up the daughter of a prohibition bootlegger and loved to tell the story of how as a little girl she'd climb into the rumble seat of their old Ford with cases of moonshine whiskey stacked underneath her while her dad crossed icy one-lane mountain passes to deliver his spirits to the neighboring towns. The story was her way of speaking of an even more rough and tumble time in her life than her retired years. It was also a warning for those with ears to hear not to underestimate her courage or her spunk.

When Lizzy was still young, she married and had a son. Not too long after their son was born, her husband abandoned her. Lizzy worked at city hall, earning enough money to keep a roof over her and her son's head. She had a tiny one-bedroom house near the railroad tracks, and by the time I knew her she was long retired; she and Robbie depended on her Social Security check and the carpentry work he could find in the small rural town and surrounding counties. She slept on a twin bed in the hallway between the bathroom and the kitchen so that Robbie could have the bedroom for himself.

Despite her own poverty, she fed the many homeless strangers who knocked on her door after hopping a train. She knew what it meant to be hungry, and feeding the hungry was a Christian imperative for her. She was at church every Sunday. She served on the altar guild. She baked pies for the church's Nordic Fest pie booth. She was a frail, almost five-foot-tall, kind, gentle, giving, and forgiving giant of a Christian woman! When she developed lung cancer, she took it in stride. There was no money for expensive chemotherapies, and so the doctors did what they could to keep her as comfortable as possible as the cancer progressed. Robbie cared for her as best he could, and the church brought her communion and healing prayers when she became too weak to come to church.

What Lizzy didn't know, what none of us knew until some years after she died, was that WR Grace mining company had for some years been poisoning the whole town, dumping highly carcinogenic material in this small lumber and mining town, with some of the most toxic deposits of all in the part of town where Lizzy's house stood. Hundreds in that town have died from their exposure. Millions across the country have been exposed to asbestos-laden vermiculite products produced by the mine, manufactured across the country, and distributed as insulation, fertilizer, and building material. Miles and miles of the topsoil of Libby had to be taken up and removed by the EPA to eliminate the carcinogens after lawsuits finally forced the closure of the mine. Friends, like Lizzy, were lost to vicious lung cancers, while the ravenous greed of a few corporate officers, never convicted of a crime, was being fed. Lizzy, our sister Lizzy, needed an advocate. Lizzy needed to be tended and befriended so that she would not be invisible in her suffering and her pain. Lizzy's story is not an isolated story. There are still many, many people like Lizzy in Libby and in the world paying the price for others' greed. Might we become advocates for them?

Ash Wednesday

Isaiah 58

Shout out, do not hold back!
Lift up your voice like a trumpet!
Announce to my people their rebellion,
    to the house of Jacob their sins.
Yet day after day they seek me
    and delight to know my ways,
as if they were a nation that practiced righteousness
    and did not forsake the ordinance of their God;
they ask of me righteous judgements,
    they delight to draw near to God.
"Why do we fast, but you do not see?
Why humble ourselves, but you do not notice?"
Look, you serve your own interest on your fast-day,
    and oppress all your workers.
Look, you fast only to quarrel and to fight
    and to strike with a wicked fist.
Such fasting as you do today
    will not make your voice heard on high.
Is such the fast that I choose,
    a day to humble oneself?
Is it to bow down the head like a bulrush,
    and to lie in sackcloth and ashes?

Will you call this a fast,
    a day acceptable to our God?

Is not this the fast that I choose:
    to loose the bonds of injustice,
    to undo the thongs of the yoke,
to let the oppressed go free,
    and to break every yoke?
Is it not to share your bread with the hungry,
    and bring the homeless poor into your house;
when you see the naked, to cover them,
    and not to hide yourself from your own kin?
Then your light shall break forth like the dawn,
    and your healing shall spring up quickly;
your vindicator shall go before you,
    the glory of our God shall be your rearguard.
Then you shall call, and our God will answer;
    you shall cry for help, and God will say, Here I am.

If you remove the yoke from among you,
    the pointing of the finger, the speaking of evil,
if you offer your food to the hungry
    and satisfy the needs of the afflicted,
then your light shall rise in the darkness
    and your gloom be like the noonday.
Our God will guide you continually,
    and satisfy your needs in parched places,
and make your bones strong;
    and you shall be like a watered garden,
like a spring of water,
    whose waters never fail.
Your ancient ruins shall be rebuilt;
    you shall raise up the foundations of many
        generations;

you shall be called the repairer of the breach,
   the restorer of streets to live in.

If you refrain from trampling the sabbath,
   from pursuing your own interests on my holy day;
if you call the sabbath a delight
   and the holy day of our God honorable;
if you honor it, not going your own ways,
      serving your own interests, or pursuing your own
         affairs;
then you shall take delight in our God,
      and I will make you ride upon the heights of the
         earth;
I will feed you with the heritage of your ancestor Jacob,
   for the mouth of our God has spoken.

Meditation

Nearly twenty years ago I heard a news story about research done in the field of psychology. It seems that much of the research to develop central theories about the human mind and the human psyche had been done exclusively on men. One of the places where this held true was in the research on the "fight or flight" phenomenon which says, of course, that when presented with a threat, there are two basic binary human responses—either to face the threat, and fight to defeat our enemy, or to run from the threat in hopes of escaping it.

But something interesting happened when, toward the end of the twentieth century, women began to be included as subjects in similar experiments. The binary began to fall apart. Yes, sometimes the response was still to fight. And sometimes the response was to flee. But there now seemed to be a third option that had been overlooked in those earlier studies: the option that came to be named by some as the "tend and befriend" option. It was not a response that was exclusive to women, nor was it the only response women could make, but when women were added into the equation, the response became statistically significant. In the midst of some threats, there appeared to be no alternative but to fight to defend oneself or one's young. In other situations, the only way to survive was to outrun the danger. But sometimes, sometimes life presents us with the option to survive by seeing ourselves as a part of something larger.

"Tend and befriend" suggests one response to a threat can be to gather around us those who are most in danger and tend to them, while befriending others facing—or instigating—a similar danger. The solution to life's gravest threats may not always come through an exclusive focus on self-preservation. Self-preservation paradoxically can come through, to quote one of my favorite self-help resources, "loving your neighbor as yourself."

In this age, the church is facing real threats, and every limb of the church must decide how to respond to those threats. When should we stand in sacred resistance and fight? When should we remove ourselves from a dangerous situation? And when should we turn and face into the dangers together in solidarity and in support of one another? Put another way, when must we exchange *I* and *my* for *we* and *our*—loving our neighbors as ourselves? When must each of the individual members of the body come together with others to create a functioning whole? Often in our lone individuality, we look small and insignificant, near invisible. But together, together we cannot be overlooked, uncounted, or discounted.

Prayer

God, who called us into being and stirs our hearts to love, give us the strength and will to stand together and face the forces of pernicious greed and craven self-serving within our society and our world. Empower us to stand with the weakest and most vulnerable, bearing within our bodies evidence of what it means to love our neighbors as ourselves.

Drought

That night,
   we all prayed for rain;
   like superstitious old men,
     we scratched a hole in the dust,
     burying talismans from our lives:
       a set of keys from a wrecked car;
       a child's string of plastic beads;
       a wedding ring;
       a bleached white bone,
         strung on a red satin ribbon.
And when we finally slept,
   we each dreamed the same dream:
     that a tree sprouted out of the ground
       where we had planted—

grew, withered and died before daybreak;
   and that god cared nothing for our gifts
      anyway,
   in fact, required only our hearts,
      good and pure and true,
         which we stubbornly withheld,
         thirsty, but fearful of the cost.

Thursday

Genesis 2:4–17

These are the generations of the heavens and the earth when they were created.

In the day that the Lord God made the earth and the heavens, when no plant of the field was yet in the earth and no herb of the field had yet sprung up—for the Lord God had not caused it to rain upon the earth, and there was no one to till the ground; but a stream would rise from the earth, and water the whole face of the ground—then the Lord God formed a human from the dust of the ground, and breathed into its nostrils the breath of life; and the human became a living being. And the Lord God planted a garden in Eden, in the east; and there God put the human whom God had formed. Out of the ground the Lord God made to grow every tree that is pleasant to the sight and good for food, the tree of life also in the midst of the garden, and the tree of the knowledge of good and evil.

A river flows out of Eden to water the garden, and from there it divides and becomes four branches. The name of the first is Pishon; it is the one that flows around the whole land of Havilah, where there is gold; and the gold of that land is good; bdellium and onyx stone are there. The name of the second river is Gihon; it is the one that flows around the whole land of Cush. The name of the third river is Tigris, which flows east of Assyria. And the fourth river is the Euphrates.

The Lord God took the human and put it in the garden of Eden to till it and keep it. And the Lord God commanded the human, "You may freely eat of every tree of the garden; but of the tree of the knowledge of good and evil you shall not eat, for in the day that you eat of it you shall die."

Meditation

Ethel Aarsted lived just down the street from the elementary school in Troy, Montana (population 1,000). Ethel was sharp eyed, quick witted, and deeply aware, intentionally aware, spiritually aware, of all that happened around her. She walked unsteadily with a cane but refused to be sidelined by her infirmities. A conscientious member of her community, she had a mantra she had learned from her Swedish immigrant mamma. "Mamma taught me, 'tend your own little garden,'" Ethel would say. This was not at all to suggest that one should mind one's own business. Quite the contrary, to tend one's own garden was to take responsibility for the home, the school, the church, the town, and the literal garden in one's life. Tending one's own garden meant caring for and supporting those whom God had placed within throwing distance. It meant supporting the high school kids raising money for their band trip. It meant praying for all those in town who had lost their job, experienced domestic violence, or become ill. Well into her eighties and increasingly limited in mobility, Ethel continued to care for her little garden, growing roses in her front yard, keeping a long list of those she prayed for every day, and bringing kindness and humor to whatever moment was at hand. The suffering of her own life had taught her not to turn a blind eye to suffering around her. She lived in the knowledge that her little garden had been given to her by God to till and to keep.

One of Ethel's best friends was Hazel Walsh, a retired teacher. When Hazel noticed that her across-the-street neighbor's kindergartner was often home alone after school until evening, Hazel offered her home as a safe haven for the little girl while the parents were at work. The friendship that grew between Hazel and the child gave Hazel great joy. She taught the little girl how to make zucchini bread and helped her with her homework. As the years went on and the child grew older, the relationship continued. Hazel's garden included this little girl. And in time the girl also came to see Hazel as a part of her own garden to be tended. What flourished between them was not built on charity or sympathy or duty. Compassion had brought the two together, and it was a deep bond of respect and love that forged their relationship with one another. Hazel knew, you see, that tending gardens means allowing plants to blossom in their own time. It means appreciating the joy of sharing without desire for control or profit, but simply love for its own sake.

Prayer

You have given us a garden of beauty, of abundance, of awe-inspiring grandeur in which to live. You have planted in our hearts the desire to till and sustain and care for the creatures of this earth, both great and small. Help us O God to tend your garden—our garden; with respect, with reverence, and with humility so that all who dwell therein may prosper and flourish in the light and warmth of your unfolding love.

The Colors of Dinosaurs

Imagine the colors of dinosaurs!
   Carnival landscape;
   the elegant curve of a brontosaurus'
     graceful lilac neck,
     her gentle eyes reflecting
       a spinning kaleidoscope.
Imagine these ancient white bones,
   all the pigment leached out now,
   once fleshed in shimmering green and gold,
     living in a spectrum of orange sunsets,
       crimson volcanoes
     and flowers the size of your head,
      giant petals as blue as the sky.
Imagine the colors of dinosaurs,
   translucent pink eggshells in the grass;
   scaly turquoise shoulders and speckled
        yellow haunches
     as high as houses; and imagine how
     it would take your breath away,
       the possible palette of a newborn world.

Friday

Genesis 2:18–23a

Then God said, "It is not good that the human should be alone; I will make it a helper as its partner." So out of the ground God formed every animal of the field and every bird of the air, and brought them to the human to see what it would call them; and whatever the human called each living creature, that was its name. The human gave names to all cattle, and to the birds of the air, and to every animal of the field; but for the human there was not found a helper as its partner. So God caused a deep sleep to fall upon the human, and it slept; then God took one of its ribs and closed up its place with flesh. And the rib that the God had taken from the human he made into a woman and brought her to the man. Then the man said,

"This at last is bone of my bones
and flesh of my flesh;"

Meditation

If our God is a sucker for anything, it's companionship. Life, it seems, even God's life, is not meant to be lived alone. Life is meant to be lived in community: God as Trinity, after all, helps us understand that. Today's scripture helps to frame the many levels of community we have been invited to take part in. We live in community with the God who makes us and watches over us and within a community beyond just human community. The music of the stars, the relentless calls of a mockingbird, the chatter of a loquacious squirrel, the hoot of an owl, the rustle of the holly tree that lives outside my front window—these are the sounds of community where I live. To miss them is to live alone within oneself—not in serenity and solitude, but in restless isolation. But for all the company they offer, none of these creatures are bone of my bone and flesh of my flesh. For this companionship, this partnering, I must leave my shell and become vulnerable, standing naked before another in all my unprotected humanness.

To partner, I must put out my hand. I must offer up something of myself. I must be willing to hope, to dream, and to share. That is the human condition at its most human. We are creatures meant to live in community. We were made with the intrinsic God-given need to depend on one another. Those who tout self-sufficiency as the remedy for human suffering are aligned with the sources of human suffering. Give me a partner, a playmate, a collaborator, and together with God, we will be one another's reasons for being. Together we will overcome human suffering one day, one inch, one encounter, one inspiration at a time.

Prayer

Trinity of Persons, in your presence we apprehend the mystery of life in community. In your presence we find our truest selves by being one with the other. In your presence we learn that each of us was made to share life with bone of my bone and flesh of my flesh. Play your song for us so that

in the hearing we may become spellbound by the dance.
Lift our hearts and our feet into the ever-changing, dancing, circle of life lived in faithfulness to our shared song.

Morning Walk

All tucked in and tidy—
    our shaggy ponies brought home
    and grazing, drowsy, on winter rye,
        an improbably bright green patch
        in the sleeping brown landscape.
Old black grapes—
    wrinkled raisins on the bare vine
    and a flock of wild turkeys,
        bold and fat,
        pecking away near the road.
Pulled irresistibly south,
    the restless young geese
    circle impatiently, blaring,
        or paddle, leaving a trail of perfect, urgent Vs
        across the steaming lake.
Warm-blooded, we hunch our shoulders
    and are glad for our stout boots
    as we crunch across the yard together.
        In the cold air, our frosty breaths
        twine with drifting smoke from
            a warm fire waiting.

Saturday

Genesis 2:1–3

Thus the heavens and the earth were finished, and all their multitude. And on the seventh day God finished the work that she had done, and she rested on the seventh day from all the work that she had done. So God blessed the seventh day and hallowed it, because on it God rested from all the work that she had done in creation.

Meditation

I wonder where God rested.
At the top of a mountain?
At the edge of a stream?
In a daisy-strewn meadow?
At the base of a volcano as it rumbled and sputtered
  and churned?
Did God rest on the beach or in the underwater deep?
Riding a camel? Or perched in a tree?
Did God soar on the thermals while looking down from
  above,
Letting the winds set the course for the flight?
Did God rest in an alcove within a dark cave?
Did God rest in the heavens while comets zipped by?
Or lie in a hammock strung from two rocks?
Did God rest in the sunshine, or moonlight, or dark?
Did God rest with a dance? Did God rest with a song?
And when the time came to rest, how did God know?

How did God know all the work had been done?
Rest in creation. Be like your God. Rest from your handi-
    work, and trust in its goodness.

Prayer

God of Sabbath time, teach us to rest in your goodness.
Teach us to relax into your providence. Renew us in your
laughter. God of Sabbath time teach us to rest in your goodness. Teach us to put down our weapons and recline in the
shade of a cool nurse tree, gathering our strength, listening
for the sound of the wind and the rustle of leaves, drinking
deeply from the cool, sweet waters of life.

Three Beach Meditations

This, I decide, is what comes first, the elemental stuff:
    salt air to seep cautiously into new lungs;
a briny tide, the virgin chemistry of warm blood;
    and of course, grit everywhere, trials and errors,
        ground up and washed ashore,
        bleached out and blown away on a stinging wind.
I lounge with a glass of red wine, absently
co-creating without embarrassment.
I have the audacity to say, "It's good."

• • •

I've reached an age now:
    I wear loose and flowing blouses;
    I am graceful with an earned, more fragile grace;
    the bag boy at the Piggly Wiggly,
        when I speak to him, answers: "Yes, ma'am."

And now, surprisingly, the week I spend each summer
   at the beach
has become increasingly less about the tidal pull of years,
more about what each tide leaves behind, half-buried in
   the sand.

                 • • •

I'm watching her and her three children;
   she shepherds them on the shoreline
until the smallest begins to cry,
   not sure about the vast ocean,
   the wide shimmering sand—
And it touches me to see her
just reach out her arms,
wrap that baby up with her ample, loving, safe self.
I'm thinking of the little starveling boy—
   how, uninvited, he climbed up
   and curled himself into my side;
I felt his tiny bones:
   twig-thin little arms and legs,
   as he nestled in close.

I think, how good it would be to feed him up.
Watching the woman and her babies on the beach, I think:
he could use a mother like that.

Vernal, Utah

JUST ON THE EDGE of some of the most beautiful and pristine land in the lower forty-eight is Flaming Gorge National Monument, outside Vernal, Utah. This protected land is habitat for deer and mountain sheep, all manner of birds and small mammals, insects and other creatures. The beauty of the area can be overwhelming as one looks out on the deep red rock formations that form the cliff on one side of the gulch while the other is lined with evergreen trees for as far as the eye can see. Except for one spot. Just before you enter the national monument area, there is a stark and abrupt break in the landscape; what opens before you is a huge ugly gash in the mountainside. Here at the edge of unobstructed beauty in sage brush wilderness sits a phosphate mine with bulldozed hills, ore chutes, mining equipment, and industrial buildings, mining dust, truck noises, and rancorous smells all insinuating themselves into an ecosystem which, until the appearance of this mine, gave no hint of human habitation besides the road that wound through it. The explanations at the "scenic over-look" announce this as a phosphate mine and tout the ways in which the area will eventually be reclaimed by Simplot when the phosphate gives out. There is a promise, but not to return the area to its sagebrush origins (that of course cannot be done). Instead, the ecology of the area will be further changed by the development of grasslands that can sustain large mammals, exchanging one form of human utilization of the land for another.

Hilary Turner is a wildlife biologist who has done exten-sive study of sage brush habitat and its inhabitants. She will tell you that what looks to the casual observer like barren emptiness is actually teeming with life of all kinds. While the species of birds, insects, and small mammals that live on the sage brush flats are not as glamourous to study as other larger species, they are unique, beautiful, and precious creatures in their own right. To do away with sage brush meadows is not simply an act of practical utilitarianism, it is also an act of destruction with much graver consequences for the larger ecosystem than we know how to imagine. With the destruction of the sage comes the destruction of essential nesting areas for birds, shade areas for small mammals, and a loss of food source for birds of prey. Replacing that habitat with grasslands will improve the appearance of the scenery from its current scarred condition, but it will never bring back all the life that has been lost. Across the West, sage brush habitat is being forfeited to human development. At Flaming Gorge, it is for mining. In other communities, it may be for new housing developments or for oil drilling. The overall effect is an irreversible change in the landscape and bio-scape of the West.

Who and when and where and how will the nonhuman world find advocates and protectors? If we destroy all that is wild around us, who will we be and who will we become?

Lent One

Luke 6:17–36

He came down with them and stood on a level place, with a great crowd of his disciples and a great multitude of people from all Judea, Jerusalem, and the coast of Tyre and Sidon. They had come to hear him and to be healed of their diseases; and those who were troubled with unclean spirits were cured. And all in the crowd were trying to touch him, for power came out from him and healed all of them.

Then he looked up at his disciples and said:
"Blessed are you who are poor,

for yours is the kingdom of God.
"Blessed are you who are hungry now,

for you will be filled.
"Blessed are you who weep now,

for you will laugh.
"Blessed are you when people hate you, and when they exclude you, revile you, and defame you on account of the Son of Man. Rejoice on that day and leap for joy, for surely your reward is great in heaven; for that is what their ancestors did to the prophets.
"But woe to you who are rich,

for you have received your consolation.
"Woe to you who are full now,

for you will be hungry.
"Woe to you who are laughing now,

for you will mourn and weep.

"Woe to you when all speak well of you, for that is what their ancestors did to the false prophets.

"But I say to you that listen, love your enemies, do good to those who hate you, bless those who curse you, pray for those who abuse you. If anyone strikes you on the cheek, offer the other also; and from anyone who takes away your coat do not withhold even your shirt. Give to everyone who begs from you; and if anyone takes away your goods, do not ask for them again. Do to others as you would have them do to you.

"If you love those who love you, what credit is that to you? For even sinners love those who love them. If you do good to those who do good to you, what credit is that to you? For even sinners do the same. If you lend to those from whom you hope to receive, what credit is that to you? Even sinners lend to sinners, to receive as much again. But love your enemies, do good, and lend, expecting nothing in return. Your reward will be great, and you will be children of the Most High; for he is kind to the ungrateful and the wicked. Be merciful, just as your Father is merciful."

Meditation

I think of this as the "It's not about you" passage of the Bible. Not the only one of course. But this one is so in your face about it. Love your enemies. Do good. Lend, expecting nothing in return. It's not about what we get. It's about what we give. Taken to an extreme this can become an excuse for martyrdom. Not the good kind that's a spiritual gift given to those who refuse to cower before evil, but the kind which, when you look under the rug, is really about me after all. How kind, loving, and self-giving I can be, how I can bear this unbearable burden alone, how I can abdicate the work of making my own self in the image of God by building my whole self around another. Most of us have known people who lost themselves in caring for another. People who gave, and gave, and gave, until all that was left was hopelessness and emptiness and masked bitterness. I don't think this is what Jesus is extolling.

I think this invitation in the Beatitudes is an invitation to be extravagant in our kindness, without fear of how things will turn out for us in the story. We are invited to believe in the power of goodness to change the world even when there is no evidence put in front of us that anything has been changed. Perhaps this is a call to believe in the butterfly effect, trusting that our kindnesses are rippling out into the world touching lives, touching the earth in ways we can never dream of or imagine. Being kind is one of the easiest (and the hardest) tasks we can ever engage in. With "the deserving," kindness comes naturally. We have an instinct for it.

I once knew a woman who had been the victim of a horrific crime. Once she had recovered enough to begin to re-enter life, I was intrigued to observe the level of gentle kindness that complete strangers, unaware of her life story, instinctively meted out to her. Their God-given instinct was an instinct to be a source of healing for her life, to teach her that life was not always brutal and malevolent and violent. Kindness in those moments was the most natural act in the world. A soft word, a gentle smile, an eye-to-eye encounter filled with dignity and respectfulness. A small gesture of friendship. A hug. An affirmation. An unvoiced promise that there was a future worth hoping for.

Kindness is the healing force that allows those in the midst of great suffering to carry on. It is the physical, tangible evidence we have that God is still with us, even in life's most horrific moments. Creation is forever handing us small kindnesses. A crocus popping above the snow. The soft greens of spring peeping out from the long winter gray. The music of a shaking aspen grove singing its song of life and community. An empty seashell tossed to shore for us to find and marvel at. The earth gives without being invested in the outcome. Jesus, it seems, is inviting us to do the same.

Prayer

Kind and gentle God, open our own hearts to our own best instincts to mirror your capacious kindness. Help us to view the world, not from a safe, dispassionate perch above the fray, but through a nose-to-nose, eye-to-eye, heart-to-heart receiving of the other, sensing more than we have been told, allowing you to be our tutor in each invitation to kindness.

Sitting in Your Tent

There is something to be said for the desert tonight—
 all sand and sky and stars,
 all caught up in that long, slow sigh,
You have pitched your tent here;
and I have come in, spectator spirit,
to sit cross-legged on the rug beside you,

where we wait together for the unnamed baby to die,
where, as stars wheel overhead and wind whispers,
    I reach out and take her, a feather, from your hands,
    hushing, hushing, while you steal a moment's rest.
Helpless, I hug the child to my dry breast,
watching a prick of starlight, hard as diamond,
      reflected in your eyes
    as you wait, unable to see my own face wet with tears,
      unable to hear me silently groan for you
because you, I know, will refuse to weep.
You have waited in this sad tent, this dry desert place
    before, and there are no tears left.
The wind sighs,
And sighing, too, the baby dies.
Deserts like this can be cold at night,
    when the only light is a dry, black sky full of stars;
    when the only sound is a spirit's moan,
      the low wind keening,
      the sound of grieving because you cannot.

Monday

Genesis 1:1–5

In the beginning when God created the heavens and the earth, the earth was a formless void and darkness covered the face of the deep, while a wind from God swept over the face of the waters. Then God said, "Let there be light"; and there was light. And God saw that the light was good; and God separated the light from the darkness. God called the light Day, and the darkness she called Night. And there was evening and there was morning, the first day.

Meditation

Light in the midst of darkness. It is not that the darkness brings an end to the light. It is that the light is situated in the darkness. When God calls the light good, God is not denying the goodness of the darkness. The darkness is the starting place for all creation. A deep space with no stars. Without that space there would be no place to put a star, nowhere for the light to coalesce, and yet, so much of our human language has polarized this dark/light continuum as if only light and day were good.

What a mess that's made of things. Light, the time of movement and action and work and productivity become central to our humanness. Dark, the time of rest, of growth, of relaxation, and sleep are devalued. In European languages, the color of Northern European skin becomes associated with this good light and the beautiful darkness of most human beings is cast as a shadow humanness through its association with darkness and night. Good days are light and bright. Bad days are dark and gloomy. Truth shines in the light. Evil lurks in the shadows. Life teems in the sea's crystal blue waters but beware of what lies in the darkness of the deep. When suffering comes, we call these dark days. When joy comes, it comes in the morning.

How might our world be different? How might our vision be changed if we chose to love darkness? Black is beautiful! Black is beautiful. It is the space for possibilities. The space where all of life begins. It is also the space of the resurrection. It is the time in which Christ rose from the dead, living, breathing, communing with God in peace; waiting for humans to arise and find him alive and triumphant. The triumph of Easter came in the night. In the darkness. The light made that triumph visible to the human world, but even before then stars and angels already caroled their nighttime songs of birth and rebirth.

Prayer

Holy darkness, sweet silent darkness, let us not be afraid to enter you. Darkness is our womb of safety. Our place of possibility. Darkness cradles our moments of deepest intimacy when the blinding lights of busyness recede and all that's left to listen for is the steady heartbeat of a sleeping world, as we are slowly, effortlessly inhaling and exhaling the invisible black matter that forms us all into translucent stardust.

Sleeping on the Beach
(before another moon launch)

Curled like commas
   in the white sand, we slept
   on the eve of another launch, dreaming
     maybe of when we were born,
     tumbling downward on the rhythmic waves
       of our mothers' wombs—
     thrust out finally into daylight.
Waking was like birth—
   or like gravity after walking on the moon.
And beaded with salt dew
   at the ocean's edge, we stood newborn
   in primal morning, looking up,
     our long shadows like exclamations
     stretching out behind us—
       as we watched another moon launch;
       as we watched astronauts, like infants,
         thrust out into night.

Tuesday

Genesis 1:6–8

And God said, "Let there be a dome in the midst of the waters, and let it separate the waters from the waters." So God made the dome and separated the waters that were under the dome from the waters that were above the dome. And it was so. God called the dome Sky. And there was evening and there was morning, the second day.

Meditation

God made a stratosphere, a way of protecting the earth from the heat generated by the intensity of light. The stratosphere is, it seems, a bridge between two worlds. It's the place where the ozone layer is located, and where weather forms itself. It is a protective shield for us who came to be beneath it. A kind friend to be cherished. Sky. Witnesses have told me that the sky above my house was once so polluted with the byproducts of fossil fuel burning that all one could see was a thick gray haze. No clouds, no stars; just a thick gray fog of human byproducts excreted from our most avaricious selves. Snowcapped mountains became invisible, along with the blue of the distant sea. Acid rain fell, burning plants and trees even while offering much-needed water to sustain them.

I fear a return to those days and what might lie beyond them. I fear provoking the wrath of the planet that hosts us as our actions bring this creation of God to extinction. Sky gives us our horizon. It shows us what's beyond our own tiny gardens. It invites us upward, onward, and outward to what lies beyond us. If the stratosphere is a bridge between two worlds and it is destroyed, which world, I ask, will come to an end? The world of the waters below the dome or the vast expansive world above it? I will pray for the stratosphere as my friend and also for my enemies (including those within myself) whose callousness may destroy her.

Prayer

Creator of the universe and all that lies beyond her, protect this fragile earth from hands that in their shortsightedness would destroy the very fabric of our lives. Help us to see in the sky the truth of our own smallness and the brutal reality of our capacities to destroy what you have made. Faith calls us to think, to speak, to act in accordance with our rightful place as sharers, not owners, of all that we can see. Make of us, O God, a holy and faithful people.

We Look Up

We look up at the night sky;
we hold our faces up,
   letting the stardust settle,
        sift down, light years old.
We look up, held fast by gravity,
never suspecting the storms
   raging within and around us
        where we stand.

Motionless, we are roaring
across the universe;
    we cling to a projectile planet,
        flung out, unaware.
We look up;
we hold our faces up
    as ancient stardust sifts through;
        we are not as solid as we think.

Wednesday

Genesis 1:9–13

And God said, "Let the waters under the sky be gathered together into one place, and let the dry land appear." And it was so. God called the dry land Earth, and the waters that were gathered together God called Seas. And God saw that it was good. Then God said, "Let the earth put forth vegetation: plants yielding seed, and fruit trees of every kind on earth that bear fruit with the seed in it." And it was so. The earth brought forth vegetation: plants yielding seed of every kind, and trees of every kind bearing fruit with the seed in it. And God saw that it was good. And there was evening and there was morning, the third day.

Meditation

Desertification. In some settings, it means that we have lost our trees and native species, giving them up for hard surfaces of concrete and gravel. That's what it means to lose plants and trees; to take away the invigorating greens of spring, the revitalizing shade of summer, the wondrous colors of fall. There is in the plant world a gentle reminder to us all to attend to more than just ourselves. The rustle of tall grass. The cool shadow of a pine tree. The bounce of a bush branch that hides a bird's nest in its interior. They each call us out of ourselves, out of our inner machinations, calling us to pay attention to the world around us.

While it's true that sometimes we can't see the forest for the trees, sometimes we can't see the trees for the buildings. Then we can forget that humans are not the only creatures who inhabit this planet, and even, that I in my bricks-and-mortar interior world of thoughts and opinions am not the only human to be taken into account. Life lived in hard surfaces has the potential to harden us too. To harden our hearts to the pain around us. To harden our ideas into impenetrable walls. To harden our words, because there is nothing soft for them to bounce off of except the soft bodies of the human beings they are launched at. Can we desertify ourselves in the same way at the same time that we desertify our lands?

In some places, desertification means that women walk miles in the scorching heat just to find water to cook what they can afford to eat. Their herds are gone because there is no grass. Their shelter from the blazing sun no longer provides protection. It, too, has died from lack of water or long ago been cut down for firewood. Life without the plants of the earth to feed us, to shelter us, to inspire us, and to warn us of what is to come. That life would be lifeless for us all.

Prayer

God of photosynthesis; you never cease your work of forming and reforming, creating and recreating, sustaining and protecting this fragile world which you have fashioned. God of palm tree and spruce, buttercup and daisy, sage brush and baobab. God of moss and lichens and fungi. God of sandspurs and wheat grains. God of plant and seed and fruit of every kind: Let the earth be fruitful! Let orchid and seagrass and cryptobiotic soil thrive! Let plants breathe. Let flora flourish; so that the earth may be perfumed with the humus-filled fragrances of life-sustaining life.

The Bird Tree

The Bird Tree is greening again this spring,
calling the birds to it,
    And wintering in a rainforest somewhere,
    a thousand brown hatchlings,
      the Tree's mark upon them,
      re-printed in a thousand
        spiraling strands of DNA,
          begin to dream of flying home.

Thursday

Genesis 1:14–19

> And God said, "Let there be lights in the dome of the sky to separate the day from the night; and let them be for signs and for seasons and for days and years, and let them be lights in the dome of the sky to give light upon the earth." And it was so. God made the two great lights—the greater light to rule the day and the lesser light to rule the night—and the stars. God set them in the dome of the sky to give light upon the earth, to rule over the day and over the night, and to separate the light from the darkness. And God saw that it was good. And there was evening and there was morning, the fourth day.

Meditation

Whatever measure God uses to tell time, earthly time has come to be understood through the magnificent domes in Earth's sky. Days, months, years are all created out of the movements of heavenly bodies above our heads. Plants, animals, and humans alike are all guided by these great bodies of light and their pulls upon our bodies. As the moon rotates around the earth, the earth around the sun, and the sun moves in synchronism with the stars, time marches on. Time allows us to number our days and to give thanks in our rising up for each of them. Time gives us hope that the seasons in which we are mired are not eternal. Time aids our recollection of the most treasured moments of our lives, so that we can re-member them, re-claim them, and allow them to form and re-form us to meet the days ahead.

As we prepare to remember the holy time of Easter, let us attend to the song of the universe, warning us that God's time is eternal, but our time is finite. Dare we fathom a day when we'll run out of time? When our last best efforts to save the world as we know it prove too little too late? What good will remembering do if there is no future to remember in? Dare we test the meaning of eternal life by destroying the world in which life began? How will the saints weep when the gates of heaven are closed because there is no one left to enter them?

For those who watched, the eclipse of 2017 offered joy and awe. The lights of the heavens were dancing a dance to which we had front seats. Choreographed, predictable, and benevolent, what we witnessed was a *pas de deux* of graceful beauty. It was our capacities to imagine this day, to calculate it, to prepare for it that kept us from fear and opened our hearts to this moment of wonder. This ballet in the heavens was a reminder that the universe lives as our lover coaxing us into our best selves, deeper into the dance of life and eternity. If only! If only, we say yes!

Prayer

Brother Sun and Sister Moon, make us conscious of the time. Quicken our thoughts to these passing moments full of *kairos* and immediacy. Help us to think, speak, and act in this moment, before the time has passed when we can be the agents of your time. Brother Sun and Sister Moon, make us mindful of the passing days; the gifts of seasons

past which can only belong to the future if we attend to the
here and the now with intentionality and mindfulness.

Almanac Time

She went by almanac time:
    the migration of birds;
    the length of days;
    the phases of the moon . . .
        (I call it a Cheshire Cat moon, she confided—
            sliver of a smile in a dark sky.)
She let the poles spin her
like a compass needle
until she stopped, always facing due north,
    the light of the North Star reflected in her eyes.

She kept time without clocks and calendars:
    days by the rise and fall of the sun;
    months by the moon;
    years by the earth, looping through space—
        (I can feel the pull of the planets, she once said;
            the suck that tells us
            there are tides within us.)
She went by almanac time:
the tilt of stars,
the stripes of the wooly worm;
the leaves of a rhododendron, curled like fingers,
            signifying hard weather.

Friday

Genesis 1:20–23

And God said, Let the waters bring forth swarms of
living creatures, and let birds fly above the earth across
the dome of the sky." So God created the great sea
monsters and every living creature that moves, of every
kind, with which the waters swarm, and every winged
bird of every kind. And God saw that it was good. God
blessed them, saying, "Be fruitful and multiply and fill
the waters in the seas, and let birds multiply on the
earth." And there was evening and there was morning,
the fifth day.

Meditation

In 2002, I heard an NPR story about the baiji, a river creature of the Yangtze River. This river and its people, it had
been said for centuries, were protected by a river goddess,
a white dolphin that inhabited the river. In 2002 the report
came of the death of the last known baiji and the extinction
of the species as a result of the over-industrialization of the
river. Human beings had managed to wipe out an entire
species of mammal in the name of human progress. But I
ask you, if you kill your god, who is left to protect you? And
who do you become without your god? If the created world
is the body of God, what fate awaits us as well?

Never before since the beginnings of our faith has the
world so needed someone to serve as the advocate for it.

Let us remember that one of John's names for the Holy Spirit, the Spirit that dwells within us, is the Advocate. The Spirit dwells within us. That is a promise of baptism. We are formed to be advocates.

To advocate is to pray, to speak out, to gather the masses of lost souls afraid of the future that lies ahead and arm them with purposefulness and hope. Never before has the Spirit so needed an army, not of warriors, but of friends who tend to one another and all those too small or weak or alone to fend for themselves. The Spirit needs us to befriend a planet that has for millions of years been our friend. To befriend a world that needs to be loved.

Prayer

Jesus, you died at our hands. As humans schemed and raged, you did not shrink back from us. You bore your own life like a priceless treasure. You lived in dignity. You died in authenticity of being. You let us lay your cold, dead body in a tomb, so we would know for all time the human capacity to destroy itself. Instead of multiplying goodness, we divided goodness by rejecting the best of our own selves. O martyred God, save us from the naïve notion that your resurrection protects us from the human capacity to ravage and destroy the body of God. O resurrected Christ, make of your resurrected people a people of uncompromising courage to work for good, dignity to live as you have taught us to live, and authenticity of being to witness to your unflagging undying truths.

Lessons

*I roamed the countryside searching for answers to things
I did not understand. —Leonardo da Vinci*

Listen, child. What do you hear?
  *The humming of motors; car brakes;
  the sound of doormen blowing their whistles
  to hail a cab.*
No, child. It is the sound of cicadas singing in the dark;
the scream of the hunted, the screech of the hunter.
It is the sound made by the night.

Look, child. What do you see?
  A jet high overhead.
It is a hawk.
  And a tower in the haze.
It is a mountain shrouded in clouds.
  And city lights.
It is fireflies romancing at dusk.

Taste this, child.
It is champagne, teacher. Fine wine.
No, child. It is water, pure, from a mountain spring.

Saturday

Genesis 1:24–31

And God said, "Let the earth bring forth living creatures of every kind: cattle and creeping things and wild animals of the earth of every kind." And it was so. God made the wild animals of the earth of every kind, and the cattle of every kind, and everything that creeps upon the ground of every kind. And God saw that it was good.

Then God said, "Let us make humankind in our image, according to our likeness; and let them have dominion over the fish of the sea, and over the birds of the air, and over the cattle, and over all the wild animals of the earth, and over every creeping thing that creeps upon the earth."

So God created humankind in God's image,
   in the image of God, God created them;
   male and female God created them.

God blessed them, and God said to them, "Be fruitful and multiply, and fill the earth and subdue it; and have dominion over the fish of the sea and over the birds of the air and over every living thing that moves upon the earth." God said, "See, I have given you every plant yielding seed that is upon the face of all the earth, and every tree with seed in its fruit; you shall have them for food. And to every beast of the earth, and to every bird of the air, and to everything that creeps on the earth, everything that has the breath of life, I have given every green plant for food." And it was so. God saw everything that God had made, and indeed, it was very good. And there was evening and there was morning, the sixth day.

Meditation

It was an astounding thing for God to do. To turn over the reins to human beings not to dominate, but to govern creation. God trusted us to be true advocates for the world we govern. To make choices that preserve and protect creatures far more vulnerable than human beings. Dominating is power over, and leads to coercion and abuse. Proper governance is not over but alongside. Cooperation and mutual respect stand at the core of good governance. Will we prove we were too self-serving to be up to the task of governing the earth; that all we could imagine doing was dominating it? Or can we still rise to this high calling before it is too late?

Bad governments, dominating entities, inevitably fail. Now we must ponder if, like all governments, this one has the potential to be toppled by the oppressed. Governance is only possible where individuals allow themselves to be governed. No matter how long it takes to coalesce, if despotic governors are malevolent, their critics will one day rise up in revolution. If humans have often acted malevolently toward the earth, have we not been dominating and despotic? If the earth is God's body, and we ravage that body, how will this domination play out? Will human rise up against human as a part of this grand overthrow? Will the rainforest people band with the rainforest to eject those who encroach into their habitat? Will Inuits and polar bears unite to roar for justice? Will the wind and the waves and the ocean deep surface and roil in fury at the indignities of our age? Will rivers withhold their life-giving waters to protect themselves from plundering? And where will Christians stand in this great uprising of the masses? Will we stick with our kind, rationalize their actions, hem and haw our way equivocating into a day of recompense?

If there is revolution, I think we can only trust that God will be on the side of the oppressed, the violated, the powerless left to the mercies of their governors. Made in God's image requires of us more than we are giving. Made in God's image tells us all we need know about our capacities to do good, to govern justly, to act compassionately, to love unconditionally. We who are made in the image of God must be the voice of those with no voices. We must be the hands of help to a planet in need. We must be the steady heartbeat of life, bringing nourishment to all who hunger. We must be the face of God renewing the face of the earth. We must rise up out of our complacency to act, to speak, to shoulder the burdens of all those creatures of God who now suffer at the hands of our unholy, compassionless human governance of God's fragile worlds.

Prayer

Spirit of truth, stir us to the depths of our hearts to lead as wise governors, to speak against despots, to act for the oppressed even when to do so will put us in harm's way. Spirit of truth, untie our tongues to speak out in the midst of untruths. Spirit of truth, embolden us to throw off our blinders and enter the battle unimpeded by fear. Spirit of truth, warm our souls to act with compassion when cruel rulers seek to anesthetize us and thereby corrupt our will to act in justice.

Stealing from the Sea

All week I have searched the shore.
I think of it as something like an omen, a sign
when I find certain gifts:
   a dolphin in the waves,
   a sand dollar,
   a god's eye shell.
I know the sea doesn't give these things up easily—
or stingy, only gives them up in a quick glimpse—
or in pretending to give, tests you:
   will you take a sand dollar live,
   only just washed up at your feet?
      Or mercifully, will you toss it back into the waves
        to try living again?
I reach down and pick it up,
   wet and prickly in my hand—
        I walk on, holding it.
        My careless sin.

Yellowstone Park

THERE IS TRULY NO OTHER PLACE on earth like Yellowstone Park, and its preservation provides us with tangible evidence of our own potential to act responsibly and lovingly in relation to our world, as well as offering us a window into the soul of the American people. To the visitor, the park seems strong and rich and thriving, but residents of this sacred place know there is reason to be concerned. When asked, "What is the greatest environmental risk to Yellowstone that exists?" the rangers will tell you that it is, of course, all of the people. Ironically, the very reasons so many come to the park may be its ultimate undoing. Yellowstone is reaching a tipping point where its millions of annual visitors have the potential to undo its primary mission: the preservation of this unique, wild landscape. The grand vistas, the herds of animals, the deep gorges, and beautiful rivers. The thermal pots and geysers. The birds of prey and majestic snow and wildflower-covered mountain peaks all beg to be seen from a car. But so many cars (sometimes bumper to bumper within these few miles) threaten all that we come to stand in awe of. Habitat is damaged. Animals are injured.

Even more difficult to articulate is the way in which a world that was never before dominated by humans is coming to be dominated by us. Tour buses clog the parking lots. Bands of tourists overflow the paths. The silence of wilderness, the space to hear an osprey cry or a wolf howl or an elk bugle are being lost to the noises of human society. In the backcountry, in the wilds, these sights and sounds still survive, but it is naïve to believe that just off the clogged byways nothing has changed. The fragility of wilderness is beyond our comprehension. The web of interconnected geological and biological processes that has made this earth our glorious sanctuary stands threatened in ways we can only assess in hindsight. To advocate for the creatures of the wilderness is to act on behalf of the poorest of the poor in our world, those creatures of our earth whose very existence is threatened to extinction by human intrusion. What will we lose if we lose these places? We will only know after they are gone. But we can know that some of the deepest goodness of creation will be lost with its passing.

Lent Two

The Magnificat, Luke 1:46–55

And Mary said,
"My soul magnifies the Lord,
  and my spirit rejoices in God my Savior,
for he has looked with favor on the lowliness of
      his servant.
  Surely, from now on all generations will call me
      blessed;
for the Mighty One has done great things for me,
  and holy is his name.
His mercy is for those who fear him
  from generation to generation.
He has shown strength with his arm;
  he has scattered the proud in the thoughts of their
  hearts.
He has brought down the powerful from their thrones,
  and lifted up the lowly;
he has filled the hungry with good things,
  and sent the rich away empty.
He has helped his servant Israel,
  in remembrance of his mercy,
according to the promise he made to our ancestors,
  to Abraham and to his descendants forever."

Meditation

I want this Mary back.

I look at all the soft, round, pink-cheeked, puffy handed Marys the church has given us since Luke wrote his birth story and I mourn the ways in which she (and all women with her) was defanged by the church; turned from a powerful lioness into a small domestic kitten. The Mary of the *Magnificat* is not some pliable subservient vessel for male seed. She is strong and vibrant and determined to see justice done for herself and her people. This is the voice of a leader speaking. This is a voice that will not kowtow to injustice of any kind, who yearns for food for her people and an end to hunger and oppression. Mary meek and mild is a fantasy woman like no woman I have known in real life, although some have tried to live into the two-dimensional artifice we have defined as femininity. This Mary, the Mary of the *Magnificat*, is a figure of courage and resilience, not the self-effacing, obedient pawn of emperors or governors. Mary calls each of us to our better selves. In the face of adversity, she does not surrender. In the face of suffering, she does not turn away in fear or hopelessness. She does not concede to life as it is; and through her example, Luke reminds us that neither can we. I think that all of us have Marys in our own life. They are our mothers and our grandmothers and our great grandmothers. They may look as if they might fit in that two-dimensional image of women, but looks can be deceiving.

When I was a child, I went to visit my grandmother in Berlin. One day an old and beloved friend came to visit.

Frau Krause was in her eighties, round and soft with an ample bosom and kind dark eyes. She looked like Mary meek and mild in her elder years; a mix of serenity with still a trace, a flicker, of the remains of the deep sufferings she had known throughout her life. She sat and talked with my grandmother and crocheted, keeping her hands busy and her mind occupied even when her legs and feet were unable to support her spirit any longer. She was to us a kind, gentle, frail old woman, vulnerable yet dignified even in her fragility.

At one point in the visit, my father beckoned me to the edge of the room. "You see that woman over there?" he said. "That woman is a hero. After the wall went up and she and her family became trapped on the other side, she helped her children escape to the West. For years now, she has been helping people escape by hiding their papers in her bosom and bringing them to the other side so that they could start a new life. Her children have begged her not to go back, but at the end of every visit, she returns to the East so that she can help others as they plan their escapes."

This frail old woman, this meek, mild grandmother, a kitten to the authorities, a benign, valueless, powerless drain on the economy. (The elderly were allowed to travel to the West frequently in hopes that they would not return and would not then be eligible to receive retirement checks from the East German government.) This kitten, it seemed, still carried in her heart the strength and courage of a lioness defending her young. What we see. What we are taught to see. What we choose to believe can be utterly deceiving. Let us not allow ourselves to be deceived any longer.

Mary, would that we were all like you and those who live as you lived; with hope, with courage, with fortitude, and with passion!

Prayer

Mary, Mother of God, inspire us to be our most courageous selves. Mary, Mother of freedom, open our eyes to the harsh truths of injustice. Mary, Mother of compassion, give us voice to speak out for the powerless; for women and children pushed to the side or ignored. For the poor who fear to speak for themselves for fear of losing all they yet possess. For the dispossessed who are not welcome in our communities or on our streets. For the marginalized, the demonized, the humiliated whose great sin was being different or truthful or daring to speak when others wished them to be silent. Mary, Mother of God help us to bear the Christ within our wombs, just as you did.

Advent

Wandering a hard road,
and with child;
they have called you mild—
knowing nothing of the fierce immigrant heart
in you.
You daydream on your journey—
imagine yourself a bell perfectly struck,
resonance round and deep—
You, the bell of the universe,
imagine one huge soundless tremor:
seed placed.

And then, there is this firstborn,
changing the shape,
punching a path into being
through passages
that will never be the same again.
The firstborn, you realize, changes everything;
for you, for all; for better, for worse,
you now understand,
the firstborn has his way.

Monday

Genesis 3:8

They heard the sound of our God walking in the garden
at the time of the evening breeze, and the man and
his wife hid themselves from the presence of our God
among the trees of the garden.

Meditation

An absurd act if ever there was one. And yet, so emblematic
of the world in which we live. Humans hiding themselves
amongst the created world, seeking to evade the gaze of
the creator. Hiding in plain sight from the one who sees
all. Using the created world as a shield as if one needed
shielding from God or might somehow find indiscernibility
within the confines of this garden. These are the actions of
children, naïve and without true guile.

Humanity has grown much more sophisticated in its
treachery. We hide now behind ideologies and rationales
that support us in our even most obscene and malicious
contraventions against the world. We build institutions of
absurdity to house the shields and weapons we designed to
protect us against real and imagined dangers in the garden.
But the call of faith is not to hide among the trees or slink
amongst the walkways of the facades we have erected in that
garden. The call of faith is the call to step forward and stand
before our God and let God make of us more than we were
capable of before our foolish desperate fall into oblivion. The

call of faith demands that we face into the storms of our own making, and trust that the one who walks in the garden at the time of the evening breeze sees us, loves us, and will not abandon us to our own well-deserved life consequences.

To live the life of faith asks much of us. No hiding among the trees. No shrinking back from reality. No denial of the peril that rightly awaits us; the natural consequences of our species' egotistical acts. Instead, we are called to stand erect in the center of the garden, looking across the horizon, seeking answers to the problems we have shared in making. We are called to speak up, speak out, and ponder aloud what might be required to mend what is broken. We are called to stand, with God by our side, as ambassadors of God, extending God's help.

Prayer

God, let us walk with you again in the cool of the evening. Let us deliberate together about how to make things right. Unshrinking, unafraid, let us be partners in the way you long to partner with us. Let us save this garden, protect this garden, together love this garden that now, through our neglect, stands seemingly unprotected and imperiled.

Becoming a Chameleon

And then one day, she just disappeared,
or so it seemed:
only those closest to her understood the complex science
    involved in

learning how to become a chameleon in the world;
of letting every hue diffuse upward,
of being the color of the landscape.
Transparent as drinking water on the surface,
but with subcutaneous storms
at work just below (hurricanes the color of dead leaves
and moss, sky and dirt),
she went on unnoticed, blended in:
it is self-preservation, she reasoned;
it is temporary, she suggested;
it is a passage, she rationalized,
from color to color.

Tuesday

Genesis 3:9–24

But the Lord God called to the man, and said to him, "Where are you?" He said, "I heard the sound of you in the garden, and I was afraid, because I was naked; and I hid myself." He said, "Who told you that you were naked? Have you eaten from the tree of which I commanded you not to eat?" The man said, "The woman whom you gave to be with me, she gave me fruit from the tree, and I ate." Then the Lord God said to the woman, "What is this that you have done?" The woman said, "The serpent tricked me, and I ate." The Lord God said to the serpent,

"Because you have done this,
    cursed are you among all animals
    and among all wild creatures;
upon your belly you shall go,
    and dust you shall eat
    all the days of your life.
I will put enmity between you and the woman,
    and between your offspring and hers;
he will strike your head,
    and you will strike his heel."
To the woman he said,
"I will greatly increase your pangs in childbearing;
    in pain you shall bring forth children,
yet your desire shall be for your husband,
    and he shall rule over you."

And to the man he said,
"Because you have listened to the voice of your wife,
    and have eaten of the tree
about which I commanded you,
    'You shall not eat of it,'
cursed is the ground because of you;
    in toil you shall eat of it all the days of your life;
thorns and thistles it shall bring forth for you;
    and you shall eat the plants of the field.
By the sweat of your face
    you shall eat bread
until you return to the ground,
    for out of it you were taken;
you are dust,
    and to dust you shall return."

The man named his wife Eve, because she was the mother of all who live. And the Lord God made garments of skins for the man and for his wife, and clothed them.

Then the Lord God said, "See, the man has become like one of us, knowing good and evil; and now, he might reach out his hand and take also from the tree of life, and eat, and live forever"— therefore the Lord God sent him forth from the garden of Eden, to till the ground from which he was taken. He drove out the man; and at the east of the garden of Eden he placed the cherubim, and a sword flaming and turning to guard the way to the tree of life.

Meditation

There is more to us than our fallenness. That's the message of Christ. We are not cut off from God. We are not the unloved, rebellious children of God deserving only of contempt. We are still beloved creatures, small, vulnerable, and finite, even as we are made of the stuff from which all life has come and is still yet to come. We are good. Just as God created us. We are made of God-stuff. And still our being as human beings is mortal and fragile. In many ways, our finitude is our best protection. It saves us from the natural forces of entropy that move us toward degradation and expiration into nothingness. Eternal life has the potential to become life moving toward nothingness—or as close to nothing as a carbon-based molecule can deconstruct. Instead, we leave conscious life with some semblance of ourselves, minds and bodies thread together, still intact. What lies beyond is mystery. We say that Christ crossed that mysterious place and returned to claim us all as his own. What did he see on the other side? Was there a garden with an angel standing guard who beckoned him to enter and bring his friends?

At the far edges of our understanding are intuitions. Intuitions that those we love have not left us. Intuitions that God wants us to be more than our fallen selves. Intuitions that our finite consciousness cannot contain the breadth and depth of all that we are or will become. Eternal life; life on the far side of mystery. Life on the far side of death.

This life is a hope and a gift—not a curse. It is a place of utmost belonging, a place whose inhabitants do not shrink back from the suffering of this world, but race to intercede and bring aid. Eternal life lived as creature. Lived within the boundaries of our molecular being. Eternal life lived with one eye straining to see beyond the veil of death. If fall we must, let us fall upward into greater life, creating life, profoundly diverse and vast otherness housed within a universe of energy and mass and boundless hope.

I think God still hopes for us. Hopes that we will come to our senses. Hopes that we will unveil our best selves. Hopes that someday we may yet walk again in the cool of a garden; a garden that this time we have together called into being from the God stuff we once received.

Prayer

Strong, gentle gardener, gently turning the soil with your trowel, kneeling on the ground in admiration and respect for all the possibilities that lie within this soil. Strong, gentle gardener, in your big straw hat and ridiculous gardening clogs with mud on the toes, I watch as you carefully plant the seeds of life upon the earth, filling each furrow with hope and promise and expectation for all that may yet come to be. Strong, gentle gardener who grasps the pruning shears with surety of hand and sculpts the wild and wooly branches into gentle arcs of fecundity: sculpt us into gardeners. Teach us to kneel upon the earth in reverence and respect and to tend this beautiful garden from our best most holy selves.

Revelation

Something gives with a brittle snap
or the dry, dusty sound of old cloth tearing.

Or somewhere, there is a triumphant wail
as something magnificent is delivered down into
    bloody straw.

Somewhere in a black, airless chasm between heaven
    and hell,
something echoes like thunder,
or hands clapping.

Or some shadow jitters and flies—you see it from the
corner of your eye,
but when you whirl to look,
once again, nothing is there.

Tireless, our prayers for revelation;
insatiable, our craving for knowledge;
reckless, our desire to be of one mind with God.

Forbidden fruit, just beyond our grasp
as we pray for a time when heaven, split top to bottom,
will answer all things.

Wednesday

Romans 5:1–2, 17

Therefore, since we are justified by faith, we have peace
with God through our Lord Jesus Christ, through
whom we have obtained access to this grace in which
we stand; and we boast in our hope of sharing the glory
of God. If, because of the one human's trespass, death
exercised dominion through that one, much more
surely will those who receive the abundance of grace
and the free gift of righteousness exercise dominion in
life through the one human, Jesus Christ.

Meditation

Dominion, like power, is a word that has been so co-opted
by its abuse that it is hardly recognizable in any other form
now. But Paul is not speaking here of a power over, he is
speaking of power with and for. What a grand image this is
for Christians of how they are to live in the world and with
the world. Not as consumers or tourists or squatters or even
pilgrims. We are called to live in our world as people who
hold dominion; who have both the capacity and the right
and the responsibility to act on behalf of that world. This
dominion like the dominion our Christ holds is not about
drawing wealth, power, and honor to ourselves. It is about
being a caretaker of all that we survey. We choose, act, and
live with an eye to and a heart for all that lies within the big
picture. We live gracefully and graciously on this domicile
of ours. We are commissioned as Christians by Christ to be

keepers of this home and all its inhabitants. How might we all live differently if humanity saw the whole of the planet as our home and not just the small corner that exists within our self-limited horizons!

Surely there are universal human laws that call us each to that kind of dominion. Philosophers may speak of these. But no matter what most humans of the world hold as their purpose, the humans of the world who call themselves Christians have been given a clear and irrefutable mandate through our scriptures. To hold dominion as God holds dominion, to love and cherish creation as God cherishes creation, to care for all of God's creatures with the same joy and appreciation that God has expressed, to delight in every creature as God delights in every creature. To mete out justice as God offers justice. To lift up the downtrodden as God lifts up the downtrodden. To stand firm as the yardstick for measuring goodness just as God models goodness for each of us through the life, death, and resurrection of the Christ.

For Christians to hold dominion in the way Paul invites us to in this passage is for us to be, as Christ was, advocates for those within the created world least able to be seen and heard and cherished and protected. We have, through our salvation, become inheritors of a salvation that is not about some sweet by and by, but is a clarion call to intense, personal, committed, courageous engagement with a world in need.

This day in this place how will we hold dominion? For whom shall we pray, for whom shall we speak, for whom shall we work? Whose face must be seen? Whose voice must be heard? Whose dreams must be embraced? We are called to recognize the dominion that salvation brings and to proclaim that salvation belongs to all God's creatures. This is our song to sing till all those within the cosmos have been raised to the full stature of Christ.

Prayer

Queen of all the earth, you rule with an outstretched hand, inviting the creatures of this world to share in your dominion; to keep faith with one another; to live in mutuality of purpose and graciousness of Spirit. You gloat over no one. You debase no one. You lord it over no one. You care for all your creatures. You protect all. You serve all in a dominion that propels itself across the cosmos in a flying, streaking, exploding, raucous cacophony of jubilation and unbounded hope. Compassion is your vanguard. Integrity of being is your scepter. Trust in our goodness is your astounding supposition. Queen of all the earth make us worthy of your trust. Make us mindful of your purposes. Make us agents of your dominion upon this earth.

The Acts

Here is water . . .
and God from God, wading out,
wet, shining and pleasing.

Here is water,
don't just wash my feet;
wash all of me.

Here is water,
streaming down with God's blood,
from a dead man's side.

Here is water,
what is there to stop me
from being washed, too?

Here is water.
Christ-bearer, water-bearer,
go out into the world.

Thursday

1 Kings 3:16–27

Later, two women who were prostitutes came to the king and stood before him. One woman said, "Please, my lord, this woman and I live in the same house; and I gave birth while she was in the house. Then on the third day after I gave birth, this woman also gave birth. We were together; there was no one else with us in the house, only the two of us were in the house. Then this woman's son died in the night, because she lay on him. She got up in the middle of the night and took my son from beside me while your servant slept. She laid him at her breast, and laid her dead son at my breast. When I rose in the morning to nurse my son, I saw that he was dead; but when I looked at him closely in the morning, clearly it was not the son I had borne." But the other woman said, "No, the living son is mine, and the dead son is yours." The first said, "No, the dead son is yours, and the living son is mine." So they argued before the king.

Then the king said, "One says, 'This is my son that is alive, and your son is dead'; while the other says, 'Not so! Your son is dead, and my son is the living one.'" So the king said, "Bring me a sword," and they brought a sword before the king. The king said, "Divide the living boy in two; then give half to one, and half to the other." But the woman whose son was alive said to the king—

because compassion for her son burned within her—
"Please, my lord, give her the living boy; certainly do
not kill him!" The other said, "It shall be neither mine
nor yours; divide it." Then the king responded: "Give
the first woman the living boy; do not kill him. She is
his mother."

Meditation

The theologian Dorothee Soelle often wrote about strength
in weakness, power that arises out of a place of powerlessness. This is a story about power in the midst of powerlessness. Was there anyone more powerless in scripture than
the prostitute? One without home, without family, and
without honor; forced to live as the human receptacle of
others' unquenchable greed. What can be greedier, more
self-serving, more wasteful than appropriating the body
of another for the sake of one's own uncontrolled appe-
tites? We live in a world where this kind of powerlessness
abounds; where far too many survive on the castoff refuse
of others' unbridled ravenousness. This is powerlessness
played out in the most personal, most sacred portion of our
being, in and on the very bodies that make us who we are.

The power to give life, the power to create life, the power
to take life, the power to protect life. Even the powerless can
hold these powers—just as a mighty ruler can. Each one of
us has the capacity to make life and death choices for ourselves and others. Even in the most powerless moments of
our lives, we as Christians are called to gather up the power
within us to work for good; to protect the child who belongs

to us from harm. In the midst of hurricane and flood, fire and famine, bull and bear markets, we are called to protect the vulnerable; to be agents of love and of life. Power in the midst of powerlessness. Power that arises from within. Claim the power that was given to you at your birth. Claim the power you received at your baptism. Rise up and save the child from death, knowing you too were once a child in need of saving.

Prayer

Christ child nursing at your mother's breast, be our salvation. Help us to gaze into your wondering eyes and see the eyes of all the children of this world who live in hunger, in want, in danger, in subjugation, in poverty, in unwantedness. Make us determined to protect them. Make us passionate to improve their lot. Give us strong arms to hold them. Strong legs to carry them to the place where they too may live without fear. Christ child, who fled the cruel intentions of a tyrant, show us the road to Egypt so that all innocents may travel this same road and find sanctuary from the wicked agents of suffering who pursue them.

Do Children Still Dream?

Nameless dusty boy among hundreds, thousands like you;
immigrant orphan, hand raised to your crumpled,
  tear-streaked face
    in the universal gesture
    of utter despair, unbearable torment.

School girls, raised to dream,
born free to believe in unlimited possibilities,
      learning now to be afraid;
      learning now to doubt the dreams.

Bombs and poison raining down
even as rescuers pull tiny victims from blasted rubble:
      wounded children crying in ruined streets,
      but no mothers left to take them in.

Bright minds, hidden in classroom closets,
horrified, bloodied, waiting for the shooting to stop,
      and feeling the first seeds of righteousness—
      huddled, cowering in the dark—Enough!

And yet, we wonder, do children still dream?
Does this world rest more easily on their young shoulders
than on our own?
      Will the children, in spite of it all, lead us?
      Will a Child be able to show us the way?

Friday

1 Kings 4:21–24

Solomon was sovereign over all the kingdoms from the Euphrates to the land of the Philistines, even to the border of Egypt; they brought tribute and served Solomon all the days of his life.

Solomon's provision for one day was thirty cors of choice flour, and sixty cors of meal, ten fat oxen, and twenty pasture-fed cattle, one hundred sheep, besides deer, gazelles, roebucks, and fatted fowl. For he had dominion over all the region west of the Euphrates from Tiphsah to Gaza, over all the kings west of the Euphrates; and he had peace on all sides.

Meditation

History, we now realize, is most often a one-sided telling of a story by the victor. And so it is with this piece of the history of Solomon. Often in our naiveté and blindness when we write our histories, we say things that inadvertently speak of truths which some might otherwise prefer remain unspoken; the Freudian slips of our chronicles. This brief story of Solomon's provisions is just such a telling. It leaves one to ponder why this king required so great a provision. Other historical works written from other vantage points tell us in a different tone about what we read here. In them, we learn of a foolhardy king willing to strip his realm and all the neighboring realms of all their wealth, to jeopardize the wellbeing of his own people for the sake of opulence and grandeur and monuments to himself and his religion.

Imagine the villages that might be fed by this storehouse! Imagine the shared security that might come to such a realm if only its resources were used and divided for the sake of the body politic, rather than concentrated in the hands of the few. This royal dominion of 1 Kings is a fleeting dominion, a house built on sand with nothing to support it in a storm. Peace may reign in such a realm for a brief time, but that peace will end as those from whom tribute has been exacted find a way to take their revenge.

As twenty-first century American Christians, most of us sit securely at the king's table sharing in the bounty of the king's provision, growing fat off the tribute of others. Penitently confessing to God while we gorge will bring nothing. Blindness to our own complicity brings nothing. The call of the Gospel is twofold: to help the king come to his senses before it's too late, and till then to take what we can justly take, not for ourselves, but to divide and share with those outside the palace gates. It won't be enough till it is enough. But in the meantime, it will be something. Because when one is poor and hungry; something is something, even when it's not enough.

Prayer

God of the ever-expanding cosmos, God of infinite possibility and unfathomable abundance, help us to learn that in the sharing, in the breaking, in the giving, in the smallest morsels of life divided together in community, we can find enough to go round. There can be enough for all. Not in the hoarding or the stockpiling. Not in the accounting or the inventorying, but in the equal distribution of the plenty of

this earth, there can be abundance enough for all to share
in the feast.

Lessons in Brick Laying

You want a strong foundation, walls that will carry weight;
you dream of a brick house able to shelter and withstand.
In your imagination, doors and windows are all flung
    wide—
every pilgrim comes in;
every stranger, a friend.

And the tools for this are plain:
the spirit level—history's ghostly hands, wise, steady;
lines—mason's and plumb—thrumming taut and true;
the story pole—about what came before, what will rise
    up next;
a trowel and mortar—for building up, and still up.

The work for this is hard:
bricks will be scored and snapped, forced to fit;
the red dust of failures, swept away.
Your tears will salt the mortar,
and tears will, in the end, forgive . . .

So then, set your hand to building this house.
Lay it down, brick by brick, course by course
on hard ground made ready long ago—
take a lesson from that,
and raise it up from there,

just raise it up from there.

Saturday

1 Kings 4:29–34

God gave Solomon very great wisdom, discernment, and breadth of understanding as vast as the sand on the seashore, so that Solomon's wisdom surpassed the wisdom of all the people of the east, and all the wisdom of Egypt. He was wiser than anyone else, wiser than Ethan the Ezrahite, and Heman, Calcol, and Darda, children of Mahol; his fame spread throughout all the surrounding nations. He composed three thousand proverbs, and his songs numbered a thousand and five. He would speak of trees, from the cedar that is in the Lebanon to the hyssop that grows in the wall; he would speak of animals, and birds, and reptiles, and fish. People came from all the nations to hear the wisdom of Solomon; they came from all the kings of the earth who had heard of his wisdom.

Meditation

Context is everything. Surrounded by the finest of accoutrements, sitting at the center of power and wealth, it is easy to lose track of one's larger contexts. It is easy to keep one's gaze focused on the opportunities and demands right in front of us, and to see our own stature as it relates to the small worlds we find ourselves inhabiting. I have a friend who lives in half a shipping container box with no windows. If she forgets to speak of trees and animals and birds and reptiles and fish and all that inhabits the world beyond her container box, she will surely lose herself. It is this greater context, our earthly context, which reminds us that this time, this place, this problem, this affront to our being is not the whole story of who we are. This time, this place, this success, this moment of adulation is also not the whole story of who we are.

We are a part of creation, not the rulers of it, despite what some prayer books may say. We are one star in a sky of galaxies. We are a part of something that cannot be contained within a palace or a shipping box. We belong to God who is infinitely wiser and more approachable than any individual creature we might seek to know.

If the earth is God's body, God's visible presence in our midst, then wisdom calls us to caress the earth, to sing her praises, to write songs that testify to her strength and her beauty. Wisdom calls us to love the earth as our own body drawing the world to ourselves, blowing open the walls of our human-made palaces and our misappropriated containers.

Prayer

Adventurer *par excellence*, take us out of our small boxes and let us look into the far-flung light of your universe. Give us eyes to see the near infinite secreted within the finite complexity of a single cell. Give us ears to hear the music of the galaxies in the song of a nightingale. Give us lips to taste the full fruits of life itself in the first sweet burst of juice enclosed within a single ripe pear. Adventurer *par excellence,* let us live with an eye to the oceans floor where octopuses feel their way along the caverns of the deep; and the heavens above where peregrines perch on snowy palisades of ancient rock. Let us choose from our hearts, hearts gratefully filled with the beauty of new snow scattered like perfect diamonds at our feet. Let us act from a place of wisdom where all life is known, and held, and cherished by our choices.

Springtide

Four herons flying.
Willow wands like green glass beads
on a pale white string.

Bluff, Utah

IN THE NORTHWEST CORNER of Utah on the Navajo nation there are two towns, each with a mission church. Bluff has the larger of the two. Built in the 1940s, the community of St. Christopher's nestles under a red rock cliff looking out on the open expanse of the Utah prairie at the edge of Bears Ears National Monument. The complex includes an A-frame church, a rectory, and a historic adobe guest house. There is a small cemetery on the grounds where loved ones are buried, from infant children to elders. There is also an enclosed outdoor chapel that contains the grave of the first priest to serve St. Christopher's along with a small Mary shrine. In the back, in the outbuildings of the church, there is a bright red spigot. This spigot of clean, fresh, potable water has become the lifeline for many in the surrounding community who cannot get running water to their own homes or whose water has become contaminated.

In 2015, the Environmental Protection Agency investigated leakages of heavy metal acidic water coming from an abandoned gold mine called the Gold King Mine near Silverton, Colorado. In their efforts to release pressure on the containment area and prevent further spillage, the EPA accidentally destroyed the plug which held back the mine's poisonous contents. As a result of this accident, three million gallons of highly toxic, acidic, heavy metal-laden water was released, contaminating the Animus and San Juan Rivers and all the tributary rivers and creeks. The rivers and streams were turned orange by the toxic soup and sludge and people were advised to refrain from using this water for bathing, recreation, drinking, or farming and ranching. While there have been assurances that the contamination has dissipated over the last several years, fears continue. Sometimes dead horses and cattle are found in the area, leading residents to wonder if all the toxins are truly gone.

The water at St. Christopher's has been tested and found clean. The water up the road at the town of Montezuma Creek is more questionable, still containing some evidence of lead and arsenic and cadmium. At some point years before this spill, the well water at St. John the Baptizer, the mission church in Montezuma Creek, became salinized, making it undrinkable. Some believe it may have been a result of nearby oil drilling, but there is no way to prove that. While the EPA views the toxin quantities in the San Juan River as now within acceptable limits, residents are still concerned about what they will ingest through the water, cattle, and crops in the area. Many farmers and gardeners have now gone years without planting.

St. John the Baptizer mission serves this community and hears the fears, concerns, and frustrations of the people. They do more than just listen: They work with the community of St. Christopher's to give away clean water. In a setting where life is already difficult and demanding, this new wrinkle has made it necessary to haul water from that red pump at St. Christopher's, sixteen miles away from Montezuma Creek, in order to assure the safety and health of children, the elderly, and other inhabitants of the area. Individuals and families from throughout this region who either do not have access to water at all or fear their water is unsafe come to St. Christopher's to get water from their pure well. Years ago, most of these families had access to water through nearby springs and creeks, but in the last decade as temperatures have risen, most of those natural sources of water have dried up, making the deep aquifers of the region the only continuing source of water.

Originally, some years ago when the first seepages appeared at the Gold King Mine, the EPA encouraged the people of Silverton to apply for Superfund status so that adequate cleanup could be done on the mine site. Having already lost much of their livelihoods with the closing of the gold mine, the community resisted this action fearing it would dissuade tourists from coming to the area, taking away the rest of the economic base the Silverton community relied upon. As is over and over again the story, the people of Silverton colluded in their own tragic circumstances. Individuals were willing to risk significant harm to themselves, their families, their environs, and to those downstream from them for the sake of economic sustainability and employment.

What the full costs of those decisions will be may not be known for dozens of years, but surely the people of Montezuma Creek had no vote in that decision and little help in remediating its consequences. It is a part of the human story that often the inhabitants of a land have participated in the decimation of their own land and their own futures in order to gain employment that would allow them to feed, clothe, shelter, and educate their families in the present. It is also part of the human story that less powerful humans and the ecology of that locale suffer all the more with no opportunity to make choices about what will befall them.

Now there is a new threat to this corner of the Navajo nation. The Bureau of Land Management is deliberating on whether to allow oil drilling on its lands; in December 2017, eighty percent of the acres of the Bears Ears Monument were removed from their protected status as national monument and thereby subject to potential drilling. Some of these are Native American sacred lands that are directly upstream from the St. Christopher's well. While assurances have been given that there should be no contamination of the aquifer possible because of the distance between the St. Christopher's and the BLM land, the people of this community have good reason to be skeptical and concerned after their experiences with the Gold King Mine and its impact on their local rivers and streams.

The environmental threats that attend gold mining, oil drilling, and fracking are not the only threats to the Navajo nation. Dotted across this region there are also uranium mines. Nuclear contamination issues either through uranium mining or through processing and storage of radioactive materials are other important issues to be addressed in the West. The tri-cities area of Washington State is another area where people have been poisoned and killed as a result of their exposure. Cleanup of all of these areas is both a major concern in our country and an uphill battle with hundreds continuing to die horrific early deaths as a result of their exposure.

Lent Three

Luke 12:22–31

Jesus said to his disciples, "Therefore I tell you, do not worry about your life, what you will eat, or about your body, what you will wear. For life is more than food, and the body more than clothing. Consider the ravens: they neither sow nor reap, they have neither storehouse nor barn, and yet God feeds them. Of how much more value are you than the birds! And can any of you by worrying add a single hour to your span of life? If then you are not able to do so small a thing as that, why do you worry about the rest? Consider the lilies, how they grow: they neither toil nor spin; yet I tell you, even Solomon in all his glory was not clothed like one of these. But if God so clothes the grass of the field, which is alive today and tomorrow is thrown into the oven, how much more will he clothe you—you of little faith! And do not keep striving for what you are to eat and what you are to drink, and do not keep worrying. For it is the nations of the world that strive after all these things, and your Mother knows that you need them. Instead, strive for God's realm, and these things will be given to you as well."

Meditation

Okay, let's be real. This is great sentiment for someone with a wallet full of cash and a giant box store down the street. For us, yes, if we would focus our energies on the things we should be truly anxious about in life, the world would be a better place. If I spent as much time working to protect the needs of the poor as I do picking out a pot roast, the world might be a better place. For me, this passage is descriptive. I am as cared for as the lilies of the field; for others, even those for whom Luke was most concerned, this passage is aspirational. It is a call to people of faith to live as God lives, to care for the small, the powerless, the vulnerable with the same passion and compassion which God shows. Even when we are one of them. I think Jesus knew, and Luke knew, that if the faithful cared deeply for the "little ones" of our world, their needs could and would be met. We know now that the only excuse for human hunger in our world is the disproportionate way in which resources are concentrated. In our world, as in God's creation, there is enough to go around. That will only happen when those with the most turn their gaze and their hearts toward those with the least.

When we gather around the communion table, we come for a heavenly feast. At that table we imagine a day when all will be fed, all will be welcomed, all will belong at the banquet of the lamb. In that moment we are fed, not stuffed to the gills like geese preparing to be slaughtered for their livers, but fed with enough to sustain us in the moment. That is Christ's vision for us, a people gathered, sharing what we have, breaking bread with one another in a life-sustaining moment. Sustainability. It does not lead to opulence so much as to balance, but somewhere in the balance there is more than enough to sustain an entire world in need.

Prayer

God of the lilies of the field, we pray for the flowers of the field. We pray for the birds of the air. We pray for the creatures of the forest. We pray for the fish of the river. God of the lilies of the field, we give thanks for the flowers of the field. We give thanks for the birds of the air. We give thanks for the creatures of the forest. We give thanks for the fish of the river. God of the lilies of the field, as you care for your lowliest of creatures, teach us to put aside our anxious worries so with you and all your creatures we may together realize the vision of a life with no need for fear or strife.

Studying the Cosmos

At the speed of Light from light,
the Divine stirs, creates,
and a million light years later,
I see the spark,
feel its remote heat.
    A petal drops silently
    onto the tabletop.
    Your life, God assures me,
    is as simple as that,
    as complete as that.

Monday

Song of Solomon 2:1–17

I am a rose of Sharon,
    a lily of the valleys.
As a lily among brambles,
    so is my love among maidens.
As an apple tree among the trees of the wood,
    so is my beloved among young men.
With great delight I sat in his shadow,
    and his fruit was sweet to my taste.
He brought me to the banqueting house,
    and his intention towards me was love.
Sustain me with raisins,
    refresh me with apples;
    for I am faint with love.
O that his left hand were under my head,
    and that his right hand embraced me!
I adjure you, O daughters of Jerusalem,
    by the gazelles or the wild does:
do not stir up or awaken love
    until it is ready!
The voice of my beloved!
    Look, he comes,
leaping upon the mountains,
    bounding over the hills.
My beloved is like a gazelle
    or a young stag.

Look, there he stands
    behind our wall,
gazing in at the windows,
    looking through the lattice.
My beloved speaks and says to me:
"Arise, my love, my fair one,
    and come away;
for now the winter is past,
    the rain is over and gone.
The flowers appear on the earth;
    the time of singing has come,
and the voice of the turtledove
    is heard in our land.
The fig tree puts forth its figs,
    and the vines are in blossom;
    they give forth fragrance.
Arise, my love, my fair one,
    and come away.
O my dove, in the clefts of the rock,
    in the covert of the cliff,
let me see your face,
    let me hear your voice;
for your voice is sweet,
    and your face is lovely.
Catch us the foxes,
    the little foxes,
that ruin the vineyards—
    for our vineyards are in blossom."
My beloved is mine and I am his;
    he pastures his flock among the lilies.

Until the day breathes
and the shadows flee,
turn, my beloved, be like a gazelle
or a young stag on the cleft mountains.

Meditation

His intention towards me was love. If only that were always true. If only we lived in a world where women were seen with eyes of love, touched with hands of love, embraced with arms of love. Sometimes we pretend that is what the world is like, because it protects us from the ugly truths. For too many, women, like the other creatures of the earth, were made to be dominated and subdued. They are pawns in wars' ugly games. They are trophies to be won. They are specimens to be studied, not with appreciation and delight but with scalpel-like objectivity designed to dissect their essence and assess their net worth—a worth that will always be assessed as less than enough to make them worthy of honor, or respect, admiration, or imitation, compassion or love.

True love is only possible in mutuality. I cannot coerce love from another, nor can it be coerced from me. It must be given freely without strings and equivocations. God does not say, "I will love you if you will serve me." God says, "I will love you and you are welcome to love me in return."

As long as one woman on this earth lives in fear, in objectification, in denigration simply because she is a woman, we will need this passage to remind us that we cannot rest until all understand that his intentions toward her must be love.

Prayer

Mother God, you are indeed our God. Mother God, how can we know you unless we look deep within ourselves? Your true strength is not a strength of size. Your deep wisdom is not cloaked in honorifics. Your immeasurable power is not paraded on the streets with pomp and circumstance. Mother God, we need you. We need a God who has not been corrupted by size or pomp or unearned honorifics. We need you as a battered child needs a loving mother. We need you as a weary worker needs the shade of a tree. We need you as an invisible old woman needs a spotlight in which to stand so that she can be seen and heard and known and once again be loved. Mother God, may our intentions toward you and all who are like you, be love.

The Departed

The house has settled now:
still, empty,
abandoned in a rush—
door ajar,
cold dinner on the table,
curtains left to yellow
      in open windows.
The house is silent now:
not waiting for anyone's return,
not listening for a step on the stair.
No light in the dark
to reveal what remains:
an unmade bed, the splintered bathroom mirror,

hanging from a hinge . . .
The house rests now,
its walls, like arms, through holding in
a history of hurt, angry echoes.
Only glimpses left:
the overturned chair,
a shattered vase on the living room floor,
        her wedding ring beside the kitchen sink.

Tuesday

Song of Solomon 8:5–7

Who is that coming up from the wilderness,
    leaning upon her beloved?
Under the apple tree I awakened you.
There your mother was in labor with you;
    there she who bore you was in labor.
Set me as a seal upon your heart,
    as a seal upon your arm;
for love is strong as death,
    passion fierce as the grave.
Its flashes are flashes of fire,
    a raging flame.
Many waters cannot quench love,
    neither can floods drown it.
If one offered for love
    all the wealth of one's house,
    it would be utterly scorned.

Meditation

The wilderness is a place to learn love. I wonder if love will
end when we run out of wilderness. In the wilderness life
is, well, wilder. Less tame, less controlled, less manageable.
In the wilderness, we take in the immensity of all that is.
Beyond the lights of the city, we see our Milky Way. We listen for the sound of bird calls and owl hoots. We smell the
sweet smells of pine and sage and wet earth. In the wilder-

ness we are reminded of the colors of life, the soft greens of turning larch, the deep olives of an evergreen forest, the bright yellows of aspen leaves on a warm sunny day, the deep pumpkin golds of an oak grove in late fall. In the wilderness, there are rivers that course and brooks that babble and geese that fly overhead honking their announcement that winter is close at hand. In the wilderness, bears grub for bugs and moose protect their babies. The skies open up and up and out and out and out to frame us as small colorful dancers on a grand horizon. Our eyes open and our hearts swell to make room for more; more mystery, more beauty, more hopefulness. In such a place we can let go of ourselves and find love, a love that lets us rest our head on each other's shoulders, rest easy and breathe deeply. The wilderness is a place to learn love.

Prayer

God of mountains and deserts, deep woods and craggy peaks, center us, not as the center of all that is, but center us within ourselves as one small tiny voice at the edge of the wild. Make us mindful of our station as we sit and rest in the vast emptiness of the wilderness of our own souls. Remind us that your love is not conditioned by our utility or productiveness or net worth. In the beauty of the wilderness, quicken our hearts to the joyous, purposeless, essence of life lived freely, serenely, and wholly grounded in you. God of mountains and deserts, deep woods and craggy peaks, send us into the wilderness to listen for the call of the wild.

The Great Divide

She balanced
   at the edge of the Great Divide,
   at the slippery verge of
     shifting tectonic plates,
        scrabbling for purchase—
sure of an avalanche;
certain of a landslide, continents tumbling.

And she wondered if all that separated her
   from the frontier she imagined,
   from crossing over into the
     great unused part of her brain, soaring or
        dropping like a stone—
was this invisible line,
this fissure, thin as thread, ready to split open,
       like a yawning canyon between cliffs;
       like a buckling chasm with no bridge.

She stood at the Great Divide;
she stood at the alpha and the omega;
she stood at the crooked line
     traced for her by the fingertip of holiness
     on the dim glass between
       herself and all she still hoped to know.

Wednesday

Genesis 16:1–16

Now Sarai, Abram's wife, bore him no children. She had an Egyptian slave-girl whose name was Hagar, and Sarai said to Abram, "You see that the Lord has prevented me from bearing children; go in to my slave-girl; it may be that I shall obtain children by her." And Abram listened to the voice of Sarai. So, after Abram had lived for ten years in the land of Canaan, Sarai, Abram's wife, took Hagar the Egyptian, her slave-girl, and gave her to her husband Abram as a wife. He went in to Hagar, and she conceived; and when she saw that she had conceived, she looked with contempt on her mistress. Then Sarai said to Abram, "May the wrong done to me be on you! I gave my slave-girl to your embrace, and when she saw that she had conceived, she looked on me with contempt. May the Lord judge between you and me!" But Abram said to Sarai, "Your slave-girl is in your power; do to her as you please." Then Sarai dealt harshly with her, and she ran away from her.

The angel of God found her by a spring of water in the wilderness, the spring on the way to Shur. And the angel said, "Hagar, slave-girl of Sarai, where have you come from and where are you going?" She said, "I am running away from my mistress Sarai." The angel of God said to her, "Return to your mistress, and submit to her." The angel of God also said to her, "I will so greatly multiply your offspring that they cannot be counted for multitude." And the angel of God said to her,

"Now you have conceived and shall bear a son;
    you shall call him Ishmael,
    for the Lord has given heed to your affliction.
He shall be a wild ass of a man,
with his hand against everyone,
    and everyone's hand against him;
and he shall live at odds with all his kin."

So she named the Lord who spoke to her, "You are El-roi"; for she said, "Have I really seen God and remained alive after seeing God?" Therefore the well was called Beer-lahai-roi; it lies between Kadesh and Bered.

Hagar bore Abram a son; and Abram named his son, whom Hagar bore, Ishmael. Abram was eighty-six years old when Hagar bore him Ishmael.

Meditation

Complicity is a complicated reality. Even a barren Hebrew woman like Sarai, devalued because of her inability to have children, still held some power. How shocked Sarai must have been when Hagar became pregnant; suddenly there was clear evidence that the barrenness lay with her, not her husband. Had she hoped that Hagar too would not become pregnant and some of the shame and self-hatred she bore would give way? Sometimes those who have been objectified by life respond, not with compassion but with hatred for another who seems to have even less power. Sometimes the oppressed become oppressors themselves, unable to respond with compassion to the world around them.

Sometimes the least among the lesser can only look to God for succor and support. Only God meets them in the wilderness of their lives. Only God offers hope to the hopeless. But to be a Christian requires of us that we act as God acts. We reach out to those in hiding, those who are fleeing, those who are abused and afraid. We reach out in the same way that God has already reached out to us—as God reached out to Hagar, seeing and caring for the likes of a runaway slave and her unborn child.

Prayer

God of unbounded freedom, we live in a world where women and children are trafficked—sold as slaves to be used as a master wills. Purge us of this evil that infests our societies. Embolden us to shine your light on all those who would act in the shadowy recesses and secret closets of this modern web of collusion. Stop us from turning the other way so we don't have to see. Allow to see the ways in which our objectification of another human's body, our evaluative stares and snarky put downs, helps weave silken threads of imprisonment for the last and the least. None of us is object for another! None of us is object to you. Make us cherishers of freedom, O God, make us like you.

Giving Children Back to God

Mother, search your soul.
Are you willing to give your son?
Are you prepared to thank God
for giving you this opportunity
to spill a child's blood
on some meaningless
desert altar?

• • •

Children are recognized as
a gift from God,
but we do not name the new babies
for a week . . .
    and we do not cry
    when they die.
A mother in Africa explained:
    You do not understand the death of an infant
    because you do not live with it
    all around you.

• • •

Children make good soldiers:
they are obedient
and eager to please;
they are willing to work
for food and small wages.

• • •

What prayer does a child martyr pray
as she climbs aboard a crowded bus,
a bomb taped tight between her unformed breasts?

Make me mindful of the glory that awaits me . . .
and too young to understand,
does a child martyr also pray:

> *Forgive my mother who has forgotten*
> *the perfection of my glory and the money she will*
>   *receive for my sacrifice;*
> *forgive my mother, who secretly weeps*
> *and curses the gods of us all.*

Thursday

Genesis 21:9–21

But Sarah saw the son of Hagar the Egyptian, whom she had borne to Abraham, playing with her son Isaac. So she said to Abraham, "Cast out this slave woman with her son; for the son of this slave woman shall not inherit along with my son Isaac." The matter was very distressing to Abraham on account of his son. But God said to Abraham, "Do not be distressed because of the boy and because of your slave woman; whatever Sarah says to you, do as she tells you, for it is through Isaac that offspring shall be named after you. As for the son of the slave woman, I will make a nation of him also, because he is your offspring." So Abraham rose early in the morning, and took bread and a skin of water, and gave it to Hagar, putting it on her shoulder, along with the child, and sent her away. And she departed, and wandered about in the wilderness of Beer-sheba.

When the water in the skin was gone, she cast the child under one of the bushes. Then she went and sat down opposite him a good way off, about the distance of a bowshot; for she said, "Do not let me look on the death of the child." And as she sat opposite him, she lifted up her voice and wept. And God heard the voice of the boy; and the angel of God called to Hagar from heaven, and said to her, "What troubles you, Hagar? Do not be afraid; for God has heard the voice of the boy where he is. Come, lift up the boy and hold him fast

with your hand, for I will make a great nation of him."
Then God opened her eyes, and she saw a well of water.
She went, and filled the skin with water, and gave the
boy a drink.

God was with the boy, and he grew up; he lived in
the wilderness, and became an expert with the bow. He
lived in the wilderness of Paran; and his mother got a
wife for him from the land of Egypt.

Meditation

Despair is blinding. When one is living in despair the world
becomes empty, lifeless, and cruel. Colors mute and dis-
solve. Smells are indiscernible. The sweet sounds of birds
chirping or children singing are silenced by the noises
coming from within one's own soul. Hagar knew this kind
of despair. She knew what it felt like to give up hope and
surrender to death. She knew what it was to anticipate the
loss of everything and everyone she held dear. She knew
treachery and betrayal. She knew unfathomable malice
directed toward the innocent. What reason did she have to
keep hoping after all was lost?

Despair is not a place one can exit alone. It takes help to
extricate oneself. It takes an arm to reach down and help
pull us up. Hold us fast with their hand. Then sometimes,
somehow, miraculously we can see again. Possibilities can
appear again. We can dare to hope. Hagar, when God helps
you see again, and you find that well of life, take Ishmael's
hand and hold it fast so that he too can see, he too can hope.
Despair is not a place one can exit alone.

Prayer

Empowering Spirit: Let us be the angels of God our despairing world so desperately needs! Let us be the angels who put the broken on our shoulders and carry them up from the pit. Let us be harbingers of hope. Let us be voices that refuse to give in to the murky, muddy waters of the deep that threaten to swallow us all up and spit us out on the near side of hell. Just as Christopher carried the Christ child across the deep river to the safety of Egypt, let us bear one another on our shoulders when we've grown too tired to press on. Let us not give in to despair, but together rise up and listen, listen for those springs of living water bubbling up in a barren land.

Ripple

This is just a pebble, dropped down
in time, all of time,
      sinking quickly.

This is the tiny dimple made by a pebble
dropped onto the smooth skin
      of vast time.

You will see men and women
running, faces frozen,
      searching for their children.

Or you will see jagged, broken skylines
against dark smoking skies;
      you will suffer righteous indignation

because, in your own private dismay,
you will have forgotten the immensity of time,
    the very small ripple we make.

Friday

Genesis 37:1–36

Jacob settled in the land where his father had lived as an alien, the land of Canaan. This is the story of the family of Jacob.

Joseph, being seventeen years old, was shepherding the flock with his brothers; he was a helper to the sons of Bilhah and Zilpah, his father's wives; and Joseph brought a bad report of them to their father. Now Israel loved Joseph more than any other of his children, because he was the son of his old age; and he had made him a long robe with sleeves. But when his brothers saw that their father loved him more than all his brothers, they hated him, and could not speak peaceably to him.

Once Joseph had a dream, and when he told it to his brothers, they hated him even more. He said to them, "Listen to this dream that I dreamed. There we were, binding sheaves in the field. Suddenly my sheaf rose and stood upright; then your sheaves gathered around it and bowed down to my sheaf." His brothers said to him, "Are you indeed to reign over us? Are you indeed to have dominion over us?" So they hated him even more because of his dreams and his words.

He had another dream, and told it to his brothers, saying, "Look, I have had another dream: the sun, the moon, and eleven stars were bowing down to me." But when he told it to his father and to his brothers, his father rebuked him, and said to him, "What kind of dream is this that you have had? Shall we indeed come, I and your mother and your brothers, and bow to the ground before you?" So his brothers were jealous of him, but his father kept the matter in mind.

Now his brothers went to pasture their father's flock near Shechem. And Israel said to Joseph, "Are not your brothers pasturing the flock at Shechem? Come, I will send you to them." He answered, "Here I am." So he said to him, "Go now, see if it is well with your brothers and with the flock; and bring word back to me." So he sent him from the valley of Hebron.

He came to Shechem, and a man found him wandering in the fields; the man asked him, "What are you seeking?" "I am seeking my brothers," he said; "tell me, please, where they are pasturing the flock." The man said, "They have gone away, for I heard them say, 'Let us go to Dothan.'" So Joseph went after his brothers, and found them at Dothan. They saw him from a distance, and before he came near to them, they conspired to kill him. They said to one another, "Here comes this dreamer. Come now, let us kill him and throw him into one of the pits; then we shall say that a wild animal has devoured him, and we shall see what will become of his dreams." But when Reuben heard it, he delivered him out of their hands, saying, "Let us not take his life." Reuben said to them, "Shed no blood; throw him into this pit here in the wilderness, but lay no hand on him"—that he might rescue him out of their hand and restore him to his father. So when Joseph came to his brothers, they stripped him of his robe, the long robe with sleeves that

he wore; and they took him and threw him into a pit.
The pit was empty; there was no water in it.

Then they sat down to eat; and looking up they saw
a caravan of Ishmaelites coming from Gilead, with
their camels carrying gum, balm, and resin, on their
way to carry it down to Egypt. Then Judah said to his
brothers, "What profit is there if we kill our brother
and conceal his blood? Come, let us sell him to the
Ishmaelites, and not lay our hands on him, for he is
our brother, our own flesh." And his brothers agreed.
When some Midianite traders passed by, they drew
Joseph up, lifting him out of the pit, and sold him to the
Ishmaelites for twenty pieces of silver. And they took
Joseph to Egypt.

When Reuben returned to the pit and saw that
Joseph was not in the pit, he tore his clothes. He
returned to his brothers, and said, "The boy is gone;
and I, where can I turn?" Then they took Joseph's robe,
slaughtered a goat, and dipped the robe in the blood.
They had the long robe with sleeves taken to their
father, and they said, "This we have found; see now
whether it is your son's robe or not." He recognized
it, and said, "It is my son's robe! A wild animal has
devoured him; Joseph is without doubt torn to pieces."
Then Jacob tore his garments, and put sackcloth on his
loins, and mourned for his son for many days. All his
sons and all his daughters sought to comfort him; but
he refused to be comforted, and said, "No, I shall go
down to Sheol to my son, mourning." Thus his father
bewailed him. Meanwhile the Midianites had sold him

in Egypt to Potiphar, one of Pharaoh's officials, the captain of the guard.

Meditation

How ironic that Sarah and Abraham's grandson is sold into slavery to the Ishmaelites and at the hands of his own brothers, the sons of Jacob's slaves. How tragic that we never seem to learn from the failings of previous generations. The privilege of entitlement makes us oblivious to our own injustices. The simmering resentments of the oppressed eventually boil over into acts of hatred and violence. There is little virtue to be found in this story. The haughtiness of Joseph is palpable and distasteful. The hatred, resentment, and violence of his brothers is horrifying. The cycles of oppression, distrust, cowardice, and betrayal seem eternal. The children of slaves rise up to make of their oppressors' children, children of slaves. The cycle does not break. The cruelties continue.

What if Reuben had stepped in more honestly? What if he had risked being killed along with his arrogant brother, what then? Courageous solidarity with those who are the most vulnerable. That is what God asks of us. Nothing less. For whom will you speak out today? What treachery will you seek to prevent? What hatred will you seek to break down? If our brothers or sisters are to be thrown into a pit, who will climb down to rescue them?

Prayer

Faith is our ladder for escape from the pit. Faith allows us to descend to life's treacherous places to rescue the victims of the world's most heinous acts. Faith points the way to rescue and to freedom. Faith gives us agency to move out of pain and suffering, back into hope and rest and liberation. Through faith we come to believe in you, you a power greater than ourselves. In faith we reach out to you for help and consolation and a divine determination to overcome. We shall overcome. We shall overcome by faith, with faith, for faith's sake. Christ the author of our freedom, help us overcome. Fill us with faith.

Thick Blood

You'll find thick blood between us:
we are carefully friendly—
    but not good friends.
Clotted scabs and scars are still there, over old wounds.

When we meet,
    we speak the odd language
    of opposites, attracting cautiously.

We are, of course, the children.
And there is, to our occasional confusion, and because
     of birth,
    thick blood between us.

In more comfortable worlds, where we live apart,
    we remind you of that,
    and ask you, in times of drought,
      when water is thin and scarce,
            not to make us choose.

Saturday

Exodus 3:1–15

Moses was keeping the flock of his father-in-law
Jethro, the priest of Midian; he led his flock beyond the
wilderness, and came to Horeb, the mountain of God.
There the angel of God appeared to him in a flame of
fire out of a bush; he looked, and the bush was blazing,
yet it was not consumed. Then Moses said, "I must
turn aside and look at this great sight, and see why the
bush is not burned up." When God saw that he had
turned aside to see, God called to him out of the bush,
"Moses, Moses!" And he said, "Here I am." Then God
said, "Come no closer! Remove the sandals from your
feet, for the place on which you are standing is holy
ground." God said further, "I am the God of your father,
the God of Abraham, the God of Isaac, and the God of
Jacob." And Moses hid his face, for he was afraid to look
at God.

Then God said, "I have observed the misery of my
people who are in Egypt; I have heard their cry on
account of their taskmasters. Indeed, I know their
sufferings, and I have come down to deliver them from
the Egyptians, and to bring them up out of that land to
a good and broad land, a land flowing with milk and
honey, to the country of the Canaanites, the Hittites,
the Amorites, the Perizzites, the Hivites, and the
Jebusites. The cry of the Israelites has now come to me;
I have also seen how the Egyptians oppress them. So

come, I will send you to Pharaoh to bring my people, the Israelites, out of Egypt." But Moses said to God, "Who am I that I should go to Pharaoh, and bring the Israelites out of Egypt?" God said, "I will be with you; and this shall be the sign for you that it is I who sent you: when you have brought the people out of Egypt, you shall worship God on this mountain."

But Moses said to God, "If I come to the Israelites and say to them, 'The God of your ancestors has sent me to you,' and they ask me, 'What is God's name?' what shall I say to them?" God said to Moses, "I am who I am." God said further, "Thus you shall say to the Israelites, 'I am has sent me to you.'" God also said to Moses, "Thus you shall say to the Israelites, 'Our God, the God of your ancestors, the God of Abraham, the God of Isaac, and the God of Jacob, has sent me to you':

This is my name for ever,
and this my title for all generations."

Meditation

How often it is that we find the voice of God telling us who we are when we are alone in the wilderness. Under the stars. At the side of a river. Leaning against a tree. At a bush on a mountaintop. In the wilderness, we can sheath our weapons and lay down our defenses. In the silence, we can stop to hear all those sounds just beyond the silence. In the wilderness, our souls quiet. Our minds stop racing. Our feet stop running. Our lungs expand. Our hearts open. Our tongues silence. Our shoulders relax, and we become part of something much greater than ourselves.

Moses needed the wilderness to find God. God needed the wilderness to open Moses to encounter. At a bush. A bush I often imagine as a sage bush burning on a mountainside. But what if all the sage had been removed? What if the mountainside had been defaced? What if the smells of the fire had been replaced by the dust and fumes of industry? What would have become of us then? And if one day there is no more mountainside or no more bush to be found, how will freedom come to us? How will we hear when God speaks?

Prayer

Spirit, speak and we promise to listen. Spirit, nudge and we promise to heed. Spirit, push and we promise to move. Spirit, drum and we promise to dance. Spirit, cry and we promise to reach out. Spirit, breathe and we will inhale your oxygen and exhale our fear and we will breathe with you. We will breathe with you; listening, heeding, responding to your call to stop and rest and listen when you speak.

Ordinary Prayer

COUNTING AS PRAYER: *A Discipline*
Try counting in church:
    numerical litany;
    numbers, a stillness.

RUNNING AS PRAYER: *For Thanking, Forgiving*
Running, I forget
    all but thanks for every step:
    burning legs and lungs.

BREATHING AS PRAYER: *Communion*
Do you think each breath
 inhales what God is made of,
 takes in holiness?

SILENCE AS PRAYER: *A Discipline*
A holy silence
 where, should God decide to speak,
 I, at rest, might hear.

Butte, Montana

BOOM TOWN GONE BUST. At the turn of the nineteenth century, Butte, Montana, was known as the richest hill on Earth. Its vast deposits of gold, silver, and copper brought in massive mining operations that dotted the hillsides with gallows and burgeoned the town to the largest city between St. Louis and San Francisco with over one hundred thousand residents. Butte is nestled in the rugged snow-capped Rocky Mountains. Unlike many of the towns of Montana, it has not become a tourist center, probably because the natural beauty of the area has been so scarred by the mining activities that took place during the nineteenth and twentieth centuries.

The most dramatic of these are mines known as the Berkeley Pit where, beginning in 1955, copper mining operations moved from underground mining to more lucrative and less dangerous open pit mining operations. Where once there were gallows atop a mountain, there is now a huge and cavernous gouge in the mountain that stretches a mile long, a half a mile wide, and 1780 feet deep.

Mining operations were closed at the pit in 1982 when the operation ceased to be profitable. Hundreds lost their jobs as the town's chief employer pulled out. When the mine was closed, pumps that kept water out of the mine were shut down. As the water seeped into the mine, it mixed with the heavy metals that were the byproducts of the mining process. The pit is now full of highly acidic heavy-metal-laden water that is extremely toxic to all living things. This massive lake of poisons now overshadows the Butte horizon and makes it the largest Superfund site in the country, reminding all who live and visit there of the potentially devastating consequences of inadequate management of our environmental resources.

The economic impact on the community has been devastating, and the now thirty-three thousand residents live in the shadow of an even greater threat. It is estimated that at some time between 2020 and 2030 the water in the pit will reach the level of Butte's groundwater. At that point it will be nearly impossible to contain the toxic soup within the the pit and out of Butte's underground tributaries and the drinking water. Efforts are underway to devise a plan by which some kind of pumping activity might divert this catastrophe.

For evidence of how poisonous the water is to life, one need only track several incidents in the last twenty-five years since the mine began to fill. The most recent was in 2016 when flocks of migrating geese landed on the lake to avoid a snowstorm. When autopsies were performed on some of the several thousand geese who died there, researchers found severe burns to their throats and internal organs as a result of ingesting the water from the lake. Now the pit viewing area also is the backdrop for recorded gunshots sent out every thirty seconds, designed to keep birds from getting too close to the water.

Lent Four

Luke 9:28–36

Now about eight days after these sayings Jesus took
with him Peter and John and James and went up on
the mountain to pray. And while he was praying,
the appearance of his face changed, and his clothes
became dazzling white. Suddenly they saw two men,
Moses and Elijah, talking to him. They appeared in
glory and were speaking of his departure, which he was
about to accomplish at Jerusalem. Now Peter and his
companions were weighed down with sleep; but since
they had stayed awake, they saw his glory and the two
men who stood with him. Just as they were leaving him,
Peter said to Jesus, "Master, it is good for us to be here;
let us make three dwellings, one for you, one for Moses,
and one for Elijah"—not knowing what he said. While
he was saying this, a cloud came and overshadowed
them; and they were terrified as they entered the cloud.
Then from the cloud came a voice that said, "This is my
Son, my Chosen; listen to him!" When the voice had
spoken, Jesus was found alone. And they kept silent
and in those days told no one any of the things they
had seen.

Meditation

Repeatedly in the gospels, we find Jesus seeking solitude
in the natural world as part of his own prayer life. Today's
story is one such incident. In his time on the mountain,

Jesus is changed. What did he find in that place of silent prayer? Peace, assurance, a sense of belonging in something greater than himself? Did his jaw unclench? Did his forehead loosen? Did his face relax in response to the beauty and the solitude he found there? Did his ears open to the sounds of the night, and did that allow his mind to open to the voices of the communion of saints?

Moses and Elijah were also saints who spoke with God from the mountaintops. They too knew what it meant to leave behind the cares and responsibilities of life in community in order to re-anchor themselves as willing servants of the God of life. The vastness of the natural world can help us to remember how small our shoulders are and how great the creation in which we take part is. It can remind us that we cannot accomplish miracles without the help of the God of all creation, the Spirit of life dwelling in us and beyond us.

Leave it to Peter to attempt to tame the natural and the supernatural. To build on a mountain is to try to take possession of it, to transform it from a creation of God into a human instrument. Peter wanted the mountain to contain the divine rather than merely reflect the divine. Build a holy city on the mountain and perhaps God will remain and reside there. Perhaps Moses and Elijah will set up camp and make themselves willing servants of pilgrims who climb here to meet them.

We build churches, temples, and shrines to remind us of holy moments and to participate in the sacred spaces others have trod before. Christian missionaries often did this with the sacred sites of those they evangelized. Yet does the seeming ease of access to the divine we impart to those places make it more difficult to hear the ancient voices that may still speak in reverence there? Our shrines become tourist traps or political symbols, wiping away nearly every trace of their past sacredness. God's answer to Peter seems not so much a rebuke as a revelation. Objectifying the sacred desacralizes it. Instead, live in relationship with the One who invites us to the mountaintop so that we may hear the voice of God.

Prayer

God, you do not fit into a box. No matter how the world tries to subdue you, you the God of life. You, the transfiguring God, break loose to work your life-giving, world-healing, heart-mending mischief in our world. In a world where idols abound, help us to love the vast expansiveness of you. Push the boundaries of our own small vision to see with your eyes, to hear with your ears, to move within your swirling, spinning, stretching, big bang motion. Blow up our proclivities to build a house too small for you to dwell in. Help us not to shrink back and hide our eyes from your world-expanding, myopia-destroying radiance.

Light Leaking Through

Broke down, propped up,
    old slatty barn, stitched together with rusty nails,
    light leaking through,
and the river, spring flush,
running by and down.

Churches,
    saving souls side by side,
    clinging to impossible slopes—
        Isn't that the way it always is?

Old skinny green bridge;
old ways:
    courtship, secret kisses,
    white and pink petals on
        a wedding wind.

Like it was back then,
the way it was back when:
    light leaking through.

Monday

Isaiah 2:2–4

In days to come
  the mountain of our God's house
shall be established as the highest of the mountains,
  and shall be raised above the hills;
all the nations shall stream to it.
  Many peoples shall come and say,
"Come, let us go up to the mountain of our God,
  to the house of the God of Jacob;
that God may teach us God's ways
  and that we may walk in God's paths."
For out of Zion shall go forth instruction,
  and the word of our God from Jerusalem.
She shall judge between the nations,
  and shall arbitrate for many peoples;
they shall beat their swords into ploughshares,
  and their spears into pruning-hooks;
nation shall not lift up sword against nation,
  neither shall they learn war anymore.

Meditation

Fratricide, sororicide, genocide, ecocide, suicide. Jacob's sons envisioned killing their brother. The biblical story says they were not the first. We know they were not the last. Depending on how we read the saga; Jacob's brothers may have learned better; clearly the human thirst for violence did not end. By the time of Isaiah, there was plenty of violence to go round. War was a way of life. Unnatural death was as likely as natural death.

Today we have progressed to the place where we can imagine ways to destroy all of humanity and most of God's creation, either through intentional acts, as collateral damage, or as the result of unintentional "friendly fire." War planners are charged with deciding a reasonable number of casualties in any given altercation. I think they rarely consider the natural world beyond human beings in those calculations, and may not weigh each human soul on the same scale. Would an environmental impact study requirement prior to engaging in war create more opportunities for beating our swords into plowshares?

Isaiah dreamt of a world where the house of the God of Jacob could rule without war: with peace, with justice, with wisdom. He knew what we too should know: That our spiritual selves and our ecological selves are intricately connected to our political and military selves. How we wield power has everything to do with who we are and who we become—and what the world becomes. Each of us holds power. Each of us has the capacity to, in even our daily lives, serve justice or injustice, life or death. May we choose to beat our swords into plowshares for the sake of our souls and of our world.

Prayer

For the hillsides blown to bits, we pray. For the fertile fields left scorched, we pray. For the children hit by shrapnel, we pray. For the frightened and displaced, we pray. For the families left homeless, we pray. For the soldiers maimed by IEDs, we pray. For the victims of moral injury, we pray. For betrayer and betrayed, we pray. For families that mourn, we pray. For spouses left without partners, we pray. For the courageous and the valiant, we pray. For those who protect the dignity of enemy and stranger, we pray. For nations that profit from human suffering, we pray. For those blinded by hatred and vengeance, we pray. O God of all nations, give us hearts determined to beat our swords into ploughshares, to melt our assault rifles into cooking pots, to deconstruct our drones into classroom computers and our nuclear bombs into energy to illuminate a peaceful planet. Let us learn war no more!

Playing the War

(We watched Vietnam; we watched the Persian Gulf; we watched Iran and Afghanistan. Every night, we watched from safety, playing war on the nightly news like a video game.)

Tonight, I would rather not tune in.
I would like to turn off the news,
>   go to bed early,
>> and wake up tomorrow,
>> game over, dying done.

Or, I would like to say with certainty:
> It's not any soldier I know, just a player;
>>   not my child missing in the blasted rubble;
>>   not my gray, bruised lover with
>>>   the dead eyes
>>>>   (a "statistically acceptable casualty"),
>>>>>   his body brought home in a packet
>>>>>>   . . . *a packet*, for god's sake.

Tonight, I would like to become indifferent, First World,
    arrogant, deliberately ignorant;
tonight, I would like to turn off the war;
    I would like not to play.

Tuesday

Isaiah 11:1–9

A shoot shall come out from the stock of Jesse,
  and a branch shall grow out of his roots.
The spirit of God shall rest on her,
  the spirit of wisdom and understanding,
  the spirit of counsel and might,
  the spirit of knowledge and the fear of God.
Her delight shall be in the fear of God.
She shall not judge by what her eyes see,
  or decide by what her ears hear;
but with righteousness she shall judge the poor,
  and decide with equity for the meek of the earth;
she shall strike the earth with the rod of her mouth,
  and with the breath of her lips she shall kill the
wicked.
Righteousness shall be the belt around her waist,
  and faithfulness the belt around her loins.
The wolf shall live with the lamb,
  the leopard shall lie down with the kid,
the calf and the lion and the fatling together,
  and a little child shall lead them.
The cow and the bear shall graze,
  their young shall lie down together;
  and the lion shall eat straw like the ox.
The nursing child shall play over the hole of the asp,
  and the weaned child shall put its hand on the
    adder's den.

They will not hurt or destroy
    on all my holy mountain;
for the earth will be full of the knowledge of God
    as the waters cover the sea.

Meditation

Only in our deeply romanticized notions of creation can we forget that death and violence and predation are a part of the natural order. Brother wolf eats brother rabbit. Sister shark pursues sister seal. Hurricanes rip apart islands, fires ravage all in their path, and mountains spew ash on all things that reside below them. Science suggests that the weakest link in our evolutionary chains is the one to break first.

In the natural world, our children are the weakest link, and if it weren't for the protection afforded them by the stronger and the more powerful, none of them would survive. Some of them don't. Mothers and fathers abandon their children. Societies devour the birthright of succeeding generations. Sometimes the young are left to fend for themselves. We can say this is inevitable, even natural. But Isaiah will argue with us, asking for a more excellent way. With the knowledge of God to inform us and inspire us, we can create a better way into a peaceable world. In our homes. In our schools. In our cities. In our oceans. On our hillsides. In the sky above. We have been challenged to be first fruits of the shoot of Jesse, making of life more life. Making of death a blessed well-earned sleep.

Prayer

Loving Protector of us all, there is paradox in asking your protection. Some of us will find it. Others will lose their homes or their sight or their memories. They will bleed to death in foxholes or starve to death in prison camps. They will be swept away in floods or knifed in convenience stores or crushed in a hit and run. There are no answers when some desperate prayers are answered while help never arrives for others. Isaiah shows us your heart, your heart to save the world from suffering of all kinds. Jesus shows us that even you are not immune to the ravages of anguish and pain. We turn to you, knowing that you are our hope. When evil rules the hour, you are the one who carries us to a new heaven and a new earth, to a holy mountain built from shalom. Loving Protector of us all, stay with us in this sad hour and in the hours to come.

Sharing the Dream

This child, touched
by someone who
shouldn't have touched her.
This teenage boy, bloodied,
hiding in a closet as his classmates
die out in the hallway.
This man, outcast
because his lover
is another man.
This woman, beaten where it doesn't show,
by a husband who wounds her,

but always returns to say he's sorry.
This dark young man,
alone on a dark night;
this family, sleeping in a car.

The list is long;
pain is not just for a few.
Injustice is lavish.
So when you feel like the only one left
who remembers the dream,
look around—
the list is long.
You are one among many.
It's our dream, too.

Wednesday

Isaiah 25:6–10a

> On this mountain the Lord of hosts will make
> for all peoples
> a feast of rich food, a feast of well-matured wines,
> of rich food filled with marrow, of well-matured
> wines strained clear.
> And he will destroy on this mountain
> the shroud that is cast over all peoples,
> the sheet that is spread over all nations;
> he will swallow up death for ever.
> Then the Lord God will wipe away the tears from
> all faces,
> and the disgrace of his people he will take away from
> all the earth,
> for the Lord has spoken.
> It will be said on that day,
> Lo, this is our God; we have waited for him, so that
> he might save us.
> This is the Lord for whom we have waited;
> let us be glad and rejoice in his salvation.
> For the hand of the Lord will rest on this mountain.

Meditation

The vast majority of the world's hungry are women and children. The greatest majority of refugees, those who suffer forced migration, are women and children. The shroud falls unevenly on the most vulnerable; those with the least economic power, the least education, and the least political resources. This feast that will come is first and foremost for them. The gospels called them "the little ones"; the poor, the invisible, the demonized and devalued of our world. Hundreds of thousands of women and children fall into this category. First and foremost, the feast is for them.

We're not supposed to say that. We're supposed to say that God loves us all equally. Which I suspect is true. But God does not advocate for us all equally. God has a special concern for the little ones; for those who are oppressed, who have been treated unjustly or been dehumanized by others for some political, psychological, or economic gain. Gustavo Gutierrez called it God's preferential option for the poor. Some don't like to hear that. They want to believe that God watches over the rich as well as the poor. Maybe so, but my money is still on the little ones when the time comes for this great and wondrous feast. Come to the front of the line, God will say. You feast first!

You who have gone hungry. You who have had no home. You who have lived in fear for your life. You who have been raped. You who have been shamed. You who have been ignored. You who have not been seen or counted. You who have suffered because of who you are since you were born. You! Come to the best tables! Feast in safety. Feast in abundance. Feast without fear or shame; for this feast on this mountaintop was prepared especially for you!

The kicker is this feast doesn't happen through magic. It happens because we work with God to make it happen. It happens because we choose a different way. Some days that seems so elusive, so impossible, I want to dream that God will swoop down and prepare this sumptuous table whether we're on board or not. Yet in my heart of hearts, I know that God is still counting on God's people to build the table, to set the places, to create the harvest, and to share the feast.

Prayer

By your grace, may the table be spread. By your grace, may the music commence. By your grace, may the doors be opened so that together we all may feast and frolic and sing and laugh and dance in the great banquet hall of your most welcoming home!

Heaven

This is not the exclusive gated community
we were led by all the publicity to expect:
    no high-end mansions in pearly cul-de-sacs;
    no saintly guard at the gate checking IDs.

On the contrary, this heaven is noisy and teeming,
spontaneous parades spilling out and over:
the unclean and uneducated, the unpopular and unlikely,
    the unexpected and uninvited.

Heaven is not up.
You glimpse it sideways and swift—
    at the bar, on the playground;
    subways, alleys, in ordinary company.

The fine gates of heaven and the secrets behind them
   are blown.
Hanging now by their broken hinges,
   we find them disturbingly open to all;
   revealing nothing like the promised land we once
      expected.

Thursday

Isaiah 30:18–26

Therefore our God waits to be gracious to you;
    therefore she will rise up to show mercy to you.
For our God is a God of justice;
    blessed are all those who wait for her.

Truly, O people in Zion, inhabitants of Jerusalem, you shall weep no more. She will surely be gracious to you at the sound of your cry; when she hears it, she will answer you. Though our God may give you the bread of adversity and the water of affliction, yet your Teacher will not hide herself any more, but your eyes shall see your Teacher. And when you turn to the right or when you turn to the left, your ears shall hear a word behind you, saying, "This is the way; walk in it." Then you will defile your silver-covered idols and your gold-plated images. You will scatter them like filthy rags; you will say to them, "Away with you!"

She will give rain for the seed with which you sow the ground, and grain, the produce of the ground, which will be rich and plenteous. On that day your cattle will graze in broad pastures; and the oxen and donkeys that till the ground will eat silage, which has been winnowed with shovel and fork. On every lofty mountain and every high hill there will be brooks running with water—on a day of the great slaughter, when the towers fall. Moreover, the light of the moon will be like the light of the sun, and the light of the sun will be sevenfold, like the light of seven days, on the day when our God binds up the injuries of her people, and heals the wounds inflicted by her blow.

Meditation

On every lofty mountain and every high hill there will be brooks running with water. The day is fast approaching when this eschatological vision may well be seen as a vision of heaven for us all. Over and over again, the story of human suffering has been laced with the story of water. Sometimes too much, more often too little. Water as the source of life and the sustainer of life. It was in the briny soup of an ancient sea that life, biological life, came into being. It is in the pure waters of baptism we are born anew. The water of our first cradles, gently rocking us within our mothers' wombs. The sweet waters that quench the thirst of a just-born child drinking from a mother's breast. The waters of bath, of prismatic sprinklers dancing in the summer afternoon sun. The waters that create the stews and broths that feed a famished family when there is little enough to go round. And then, one day the water turned to wine. The fragrant taste of abundance and plenty, of jugs that will not give out—of the best saved for last. Eat, drink, and be merry! Yes, we die, but we die to be born again.

Yet what will be our recompense if we taint the water flowing from those brooks? What of the day when brooks are gone and all that lies before us is parched land and empty creek beds? What will become of us then? Will even our vision of heaven, our hope for a better tomorrow, perish on that day?

Prayer

Fountain of life, source of all being, help us to treasure the holy gift of water. May wells of wisdom rise up within us so that we come to cherish brook and stream, lake and aquifer, rain and snow, glacier and iceberg, oceans and inlets, swamps and bogs and dewy mists. Let us be protectors of the waters of life. Help us to live in solidarity with those who travel miles to find water and bear the burden of then carrying it home. Give us compassion to lift the heavy load that lies upon those who shrivel and thirst in our barren human-created deserts.

Rain

Heaven's windows
thrown open—
    and blessings flung out,
    babies with the bath water,
to fall indiscriminately down
upon us all.

Friday

Isaiah 40:9–24

Get you up to a high mountain,
    O Zion, herald of good tidings;
lift up your voice with strength,
    O Jerusalem, herald of good tidings,
    lift it up, do not fear;
say to the cities of Judah,
    "Here is your God!"
See, the Lord God comes with might,
    and his arm rules for him;
his reward is with him,
    and his recompense before him.
He will feed his flock like a shepherd;
    he will gather the lambs in his arms,
and carry them in his bosom,
    and gently lead the mother sheep.
Who has measured the waters in the hollow of his hand
    and marked off the heavens with a span,
enclosed the dust of the earth in a measure,
    and weighed the mountains in scales
    and the hills in a balance?
Who has directed the spirit of the Lord,
    or as his counsellor has instructed him?
Whom did he consult for his enlightenment,
    and who taught him the path of justice?

Who taught him knowledge,
    and showed him the way of understanding?
Even the nations are like a drop from a bucket,
    and are accounted as dust on the scales;
    see, he takes up the isles like fine dust.
Lebanon would not provide fuel enough,
    nor are its animals enough for a burnt offering.
All the nations are as nothing before him;
    they are accounted by him as less than nothing and
        emptiness.
To whom then will you liken God,
    or what likeness compare with him?
An idol? —A workman casts it,
    and a goldsmith overlays it with gold,
    and casts for it silver chains.
As a gift one chooses mulberry wood
    —wood that will not rot—
then seeks out a skilled artisan
    to set up an image that will not topple.
Have you not known? Have you not heard?
    Has it not been told you from the beginning?
    Have you not understood from the foundations
        of the earth?
It is he who sits above the circle of the earth,
    and its inhabitants are like grasshoppers;
who stretches out the heavens like a curtain,
    and spreads them like a tent to live in;
who brings princes to naught,
    and makes the rulers of the earth as nothing.

Scarcely are they planted, scarcely sown,
    scarcely has their stem taken root in the earth,
when he blows upon them, and they wither,
    and the tempest carries them off like stubble.

Meditation

How lofty God is but that's only half the story to be sure. That self-same God dwells with us coursing the sweet breath of life through arteries, carrying the stuff of the cosmos made and remade from heart to palms to soles, to souls that burn with the bright heat of divine love. It is the fire of love that opens our eyes to the grandeur of the world in which we live. It is the divine spark planted within that witnesses to the utmost connectedness of a comet's dust, a planet's spin, a cypress knee, a dragonfly's flight, and the touch of a newborn reaching for who knows what, but something, someone yet unformed within the consciousness of that small child. This God of all creation who sits above the circle of the earth does not just plant there, but instead glides in and out and up and down, and round and round our body-possessed, everyday lives: this God dances with us in the dance of pure delight at the scrumptiousness, the extravagance, the indescribable iridescence of being.

Prayer

Source of awe and wonder, we wonder at your glorious creation. We fall to our knees in adoration. We delight in splendor heaped upon beauty. The heavens sing your praises. The mountains sing your praises. The oceans sing your praises. With northern lights and twinkling stars, with fragrant flowers and the lush thick smells of briny seas. With soaring hawks and slithering slugs and children's singing, the world sings your praises. In the joy, in the beauty, in the wonder of the cosmos, how can we help but sing your praises?

I Am

I am right here:
more than the nebulous "I am here,"
it is the implication of intimacy, proximity.

If God says to you: I am here . . .
or if God says to you: I am *right* here,
which is more wonderful, more terrifying?

Saturday

Isaiah 40:25–31

To whom then will you compare me,
   or who is my equal? says the Holy One.
Lift up your eyes on high and see:
   Who created these?
She who brings out their host and numbers them,
   calling them all by name;
because she is great in strength,
   mighty in power,
   not one is missing.
Why do you say, O Jacob,
   and speak, O Israel,
"My way is hidden from our God,
   and my right is disregarded by my God"?
Have you not known? Have you not heard?
Our God is the everlasting God,
   the Creator of the ends of the earth.
She does not faint or grow weary;
   her understanding is unsearchable.
She gives power to the faint,
   and strengthens the powerless.
Even youths will faint and be weary,
   and the young will fall exhausted;
but those who wait for our God shall renew their
      strength,
   they shall mount up with wings like eagles,

they shall run and not be weary,
they shall walk and not faint.

Meditation

Not to be weary—now that is an eschatological vision. Weariness surrounds us. God of all creation, give power to us the faint. Strengthen the powerless. Fill our eyes with new vision. Fill our hearts with new courage. Help us to see that somehow in the struggles, in the waiting, in the hoping, in the longing; in the prayers, there is meaning to be had and life to be lived and love to be shared and goodness to be cherished. The goodness of being, the goodness of those first seven days of creation is still ours to be had if we will but open our eyes and our arms and reach beyond our weariness. The empty tomb was indeed a tomb filled with the grief and mourning of a broken people before love could arise and reclaim the day. Help us to reclaim the day, to tend our own small gardens, to rise early bearing perfumes too costly to be wasted on the dead. Anoint our bodies with the oils of love that protect us from our own exhausted weariness. Let us run to meet our best and future selves, carrying torches to light the night sky. In the night, in the darkness, in the moment of bottomless weariness, God will find us weeping, and effortlessly, we will arise.

Prayer

God who sanctifies the journey, help us to run and not be weary; to walk and not faint. When we are overcome with exhaustion in the face of the work at hand, revive us. When we are overcome with confusion over how to move for-

ward, clear our minds. When we are broken and battered
from the falls we have taken, be our balm. For the journey
to justice is your journey and our journey, and we dare not
rest till justice comes.

To Move Again

You look as far ahead as you possibly can,
   but there is always
     the bend in the road,
     the crest of a hill,
     the last blue ridge where earth and sky lock together
       beyond which, without moving,
       you simply cannot know.

So who can blame you after coming this far
when you cry out,
   when, with your skinned knees and bloody knuckles,
you are too tired to keep moving?

The answer is:
there are no easy answers;
there is no map.

And so, left to your own devices,
you will be expected to show some spunk,
      to pick a guiding star in the cold night sky,
       and, with faith in nothing but that thin, small light,
           start moving again.

East Helena, Montana

THE EAST HELENA LEAD SMELTER has become a Superfund site since the closure of the smelter operations in 2001. While the metal was not mined in East Helena, it was sent there to be processed and one of the byproducts of the processing, besides the already toxic lead residue, was arsenic. Holding ponds on the site are designed to contain the arsenic by collecting rainwater that will have been contaminated by exposure to the soil and by holding contaminated processing water in place.

Like so many mining-related operations, the risk of water contamination is very real if the water begins to seep from the holding tanks into the local ground water. To prevent this, a 62-acre protective layer of soil has been placed on the contaminated soil. The area of the Superfund is dotted with small wells so that there can be constant monitoring for potential contamination. There could be no alleviation for the problem if contamination happens, but there would be the opportunity to warn individuals of the dangers for such time as the contamination continued.

The EPA is particularly monitoring a large underground arsenic and selenium plume that has developed as water from a local lake has pushed through the poisoned hillsides and is headed toward Prickly Pear Creek. In addition, remediation has involved replacing the topsoil on most of the lawns in the East Helena area due to health concerns from both air- and water-borne contamination. During the most active time of the Superfund cleanup efforts, unemployed Asarco Corporation smelter workers found new, if somewhat perilous, work on the Superfund. With that Superfund winding down, workers find themselves now living in a town with collapsed property values and no significant employer. Many of them face significant health risks as a result of their decades-long exposure to all the carcinogens on their worksite.

Lent Five

John 11:1–44

Now a certain man was ill, Lazarus of Bethany, the village of Mary and her sister Martha. Mary was the one who anointed the Lord with perfume and wiped his feet with her hair; her brother Lazarus was ill. So the sisters sent a message to Jesus, "Lord, he whom you love is ill." But when Jesus heard it, he said, "This illness does not lead to death; rather it is for God's glory, so that the Son of God may be glorified through it." Accordingly, though Jesus loved Martha and her sister and Lazarus, after having heard that Lazarus was ill, he stayed two days longer in the place where he was.

Then after this he said to the disciples, "Let us go to Judea again." The disciples said to him, "Rabbi, the Jews were just now trying to stone you, and are you going there again?" Jesus answered, "Are there not twelve hours of daylight? Those who walk during the day do not stumble, because they see the light of this world. But those who walk at night stumble, because the light is not in them." After saying this, he told them, "Our friend Lazarus has fallen asleep, but I am going there to awaken him." The disciples said to him, "Lord, if he has fallen asleep, he will be all right." Jesus, however, had been speaking about his death, but they thought that he was referring merely to sleep. Then Jesus told them plainly, "Lazarus is dead. For your sake I am glad I was not there, so that you may believe. But let us go to him."

Thomas, who was called the Twin, said to his fellow disciples, "Let us also go, that we may die with him."

When Jesus arrived, he found that Lazarus had already been in the tomb for four days. Now Bethany was near Jerusalem, some two miles away, and many of the Jews had come to Martha and Mary to console them about their brother. When Martha heard that Jesus was coming, she went and met him, while Mary stayed at home. Martha said to Jesus, "Lord, if you had been here, my brother would not have died. But even now I know that God will give you whatever you ask of him." Jesus said to her, "Your brother will rise again." Martha said to him, "I know that he will rise again in the resurrection on the last day." Jesus said to her, "I am the resurrection and the life. Those who believe in me, even though they die, will live, and everyone who lives and believes in me will never die. Do you believe this?" She said to him, "Yes, Lord, I believe that you are the Messiah, the Son of God, the one coming into the world."

When she had said this, she went back and called her sister Mary, and told her privately, "The teacher is here and is calling for you." And when she heard it, she got up quickly and went to him. Now Jesus had not yet come to the village but was still at the place where Martha had met him. The Jews who were with her in the house, consoling her, saw Mary get up quickly and go out. They followed her because they thought that she was going to the tomb to weep there. When Mary came where Jesus was and saw him, she knelt at his feet and said to him, "Lord, if you had been here, my brother would not have died." When Jesus saw her weeping, and the Jews who came with her also weeping, he was greatly disturbed in spirit and deeply moved. He said, "Where have you laid him?" They said to him, "Lord, come and see." Jesus began to weep. So the Jews said, "See how he loved him!" But some of them said, "Could not he who opened the eyes of the blind man have kept this man from dying?"

Then Jesus, again greatly disturbed, came to the tomb. It was a cave, and a stone was lying against it. Jesus said, "Take away the stone." Martha, the sister of the dead man, said to him, "Lord, already there is a stench because he has been dead for four days." Jesus said to her, "Did I not tell you that if you believed, you would see the glory of God?" So they took away the stone. And Jesus looked upwards and said, "Father, I thank you for having heard me. I knew that you always hear me, but I have said this for the sake of the crowd standing here, so that they may believe that you sent me." When he had said this, he cried with a loud voice, "Lazarus, come out!" The dead man came out, his hands and feet bound with strips of cloth, and his face wrapped in a cloth. Jesus said to them, "Unbind him, and let him go."

Meditation

What I love about this story is that it makes so clear, even in the midst of complete faith, that death is painful. Losing those we love is not without cost. Our lives are diminished. Our very being is wounded. Grief is the perfect arrow shot directly into the heart of the living. It makes us mindful of our own end and the fragility of all of life. It affirms for us our deep connectedness to those outside ourselves. A death that is not my own still is the source of pain and wounding. We can be as religious or philosophical as we like about what happens after death. But no matter, the pain still reaches us. We see it in the face of those we love who grieve with us. We see it in the bent over bodies and the curled shoulders of those who can barely bear the weight of all this loss. We see it in the river of tears that flow from the eyes and hearts of those who dare to feel love's deepest pains.

Jesus saw it and felt it; no matter how much he knew about life beyond death, it did not diminish the pain of his humanness. It did not protect him from the rawness of human grief. He wept. He wept with those who wept. He wept for them and for himself. He wept that the world was adrift in transience and impermanence when the depths of love within his friends spoke only of the lasting and eternal.

If we pretend there is no end to come, no moment of rupture, of disconnection, of untouchableness, then we deceive ourselves and make of life a very dangerous performance. We dare not pretend to avoid the pain of grief when all we love and cherish requires of us a willingness to think the unthinkable: so that the pain of pointless, wasteful, callous death can be prevented. Face into death as you might face into the wind and feel its power. Then covenant with Christ to forge a remedy for all that makes of nature's ebb and flow a mockery and a desecration.

We dare not let the earth die because of our own fear of imagining the agonizing pain and loss of forfeiting something so precious, so good, and so imbued with sparks of divine love and beauty.

Prayer

Resurrected Christ, you know that death is no abstraction to be pondered. Death is real and demands our attention. Death is ally and enemy. Death is gift and curse. The separations of death are agonizing. The heartache of life's ending is piercing. The pain of deaths anticipated and witnessed leaves us yearning to escape from its clutches. You teach us that in facing death we come to know the extraordinary preciousness of life. Hold our hands as we face death, so that we remain resolute and open to all that death can teach us.

Tiger and Sea

I dreamed tonight of a golden tiger
bursting up from the exploding surf:
 a powerful beast, slick and shining,
 every drop of spray, a diamond flying.

It wakes me; I look over to where you sleep,
and I lay thinking for a while of powers like that—
 force to opposing force:
  life to death,
  tiger to sea.

Old powers like that, I suspect, surge tirelessly,
 close one instant, distant the next,
 while we, busy with so much else, hardly notice
 that divine and fearsome choreography . . .

until, without warning, with no time to spare,
power suddenly embraces power—
    tiger and sea:
        terrible collision;
        magnificent entanglement.

And here in this long vigil, watching you lift your hand,
reaching out calm and smiling in some deep dream
        of your own,
  I wonder,
    is it a dreadful battle,
    or is it the most elegant ballet?

To me, you are equally ferocious and full of grace:
           like a tiger;
           like the sea.

Monday

Romans 8:22–30

We know that the whole creation has been groaning in labor pains until now; and not only the creation, but we ourselves, who have the first fruits of the Spirit, groan inwardly while we wait for adoption, the redemption of our bodies. For in hope we were saved. Now hope that is seen is not hope. For who hopes for what is seen? But if we hope for what we do not see, we wait for it with patience.

Likewise the Spirit helps us in our weakness; for we do not know how to pray as we ought, but that very Spirit intercedes with sighs too deep for words. And God, who searches the heart, knows what is the mind of the Spirit, because the Spirit intercedes for the saints according to the will of God.

We know that all things work together for good for those who love God, who are called according to God's purpose. For those whom God foreknew God also predestined to be conformed to the image of God's Son, in order that Jesus might be the firstborn within a large family. And those whom God predestined God also called; and those whom God called God also justified; and those whom God justified God also glorified.

Meditation

What if, as Paul seems to imply, the whole earth is just one large family? What if rock and tree, blossom and leaf, mountains and green valleys, and human beings of every hue and language; what if we are all one common interconnected mutually dependent, mutually accountable family? What if as Genesis tells us, we have all been predestined to take part in divine glory; divine goodness to borrow from our creation stories. While we may question the literal truth of a man and a woman in a garden who forfeit their own inheritance through greed, it is difficult to deny our unbridled human capacities for shortsighted self-destruction. We would, it seems, destroy our futures and the futures of our children and grandchildren for a bowl of pottage, a moment of safety, or a glimmer of human glory. This day, this age requires that we face our own brokenness, but also that we believe our own call to divine glory. If all things work together for good for those who love God, surely that includes all of us. It is the call upon our lives not to receive this passage passively as if it were a fait accompli. No, the call is to work together for good. For the good that has been baked into our created world, the good that the whole of creation is groaning toward. Those are God's purposes. That is our mission. Our hope lies in nothing less. We are the people of God called to work together in pursuit of God's purposes, to work as Christ worked for a world in which love rules the hearts and the hands of strong and weak, rich and poor alike. No degree of fallenness or brokenness or unseeing diminishes this call upon our lives.

Prayer

Spirit, intercede for us. When we do not have the words. When we cannot see the vision. When we groan in labor longing for a reality we cannot comprehend; intercede for us. Set our hands to the wheel. Lift our eyes to the horizon. Untie our tongues, and loose our hearts, and unbind our hands so that your will may be done on earth and in space as in heaven. Let us labor with you as our midwife as we birth our salvation, as you deliver our hope. Save us from the time of trial. Open our wombs to new life, new love, a new heaven and a new earth made real and possible by your unceasing intercessions.

Praying in the Dark

She prayed fearlessly,
    guessing she had nothing to lose
    and as much to gain as she dared to name.
In secret, she fired her litany
    into what, for all she knew,
    was only empty space:
      it didn't matter—
        she was done with faith,
        she was going on intuition, unapologetic.

She prayed privately, in the dark,
    keenly aware that answers would be vague
    and quite probably, products of her own imagination.
Why expect more now? she reasoned,
    her fierce, soft, human outcry,
    just a ripple in the darkness . . .

      or maybe flying at last,
        a psalm of hope,
to God's strange, listening ears.

Tuesday

Romans 8:31–39

What then are we to say about these things? If God is for us, who is against us? He who did not withhold his own Son, but gave him up for all of us, will he not with him also give us everything else? Who will bring any charge against God's elect? It is God who justifies. Who is to condemn? It is Christ Jesus, who died, yes, who was raised, who is at the right hand of God, who indeed intercedes for us. Who will separate us from the love of Christ? Will hardship, or distress, or persecution, or famine, or nakedness, or peril, or sword? As it is written,

> "For your sake we are being killed all day long;
> we are accounted as sheep to be slaughtered."

No, in all these things we are more than conquerors through him who loved us. For I am convinced that neither death, nor life, nor angels, nor rulers, nor things present, nor things to come, nor powers, nor height, nor depth, nor anything else in all creation, will be able to separate us from the love of God in Christ Jesus our Lord.

Meditation

Divine love: beyond our comprehension and yet planted within us. Love that demands compassion and courage, vision and hope. Love that keeps believing in the goodness of creation even in the face of vast evidence to the contrary.

This divine love is our birthright as creatures of God. It is the luminescent stuff of which stars and comets, moons, and planets are made. It is the force within that propels us toward one another in passion and reverence and awe. Divine love is our friend who leads us into friendship. Strong, faithful, resilient, ever renewing bonds of admiration and self-giving. Divine love refuses to be conquered even in the face of death and annihilation. It is the last great yes that cannot be undone by all the nos of our story. If our efforts fail. If we've waited too long. If our purposefulness grows weak. If our courage to right the wrongs of our day, and our all too checkered past, gives out. If oppression continues and mayhem follows. If chaos reigns. If the forces of evil surround our world with plumes of toxic gas and poison rain, still divine love will be there. God will not abandon us, even if we lose heart and abandon ourselves. To the last, to the last breath of the last faithful creature, God's divine love will be there, and somehow, somewhere, someway that love will spark, leading the last of our great family forward into ever-growing love. It is a paradox, is it not, that we are called first and foremost to work for the kingdom of God, to renew the face of the earth; and yet, no matter how small or how great our efforts may prove to be, it is love that will have the last word.

Prayer 35

God of love, we will live in love. God of love, we will hope in love. God of love, we will keep faith in love. God of love, let love be the last word.

Pentecost

Consider the illusion of solidity:
    that table, nothing but atoms hovering,
    you as you lift a cup of tea, nothing but whirling
        quarks, repulsed by one another;
        yet still held together somehow—
            held together by some holy binding breath
            between particles.

I, with all of creation: tables, cups of tea, you—
wait on Pentecost,
    wait for spirit,
        charged and dancing,
        to come down,
            permeate, fill the spaces
            in between.

And while I wait, I touch you,
    and would fall through
    were it not for spirit;
        would sink into some molecular soup of our
        faces, limbs and hearts . . .

were it not for spirit,
holy gravity,
holding us together . . .
        and apart.

Wednesday

1 Corinthians 4:1–2, 8–13

Think of us in this way, as servants of Christ and stewards of God's mysteries. Moreover, it is required of stewards that they should be found trustworthy.

Already you have all you want! Already you have become rich! Quite apart from us you have become royalty! Indeed, I wish that you had become royalty, so that we might be royal with you! For I think that God has exhibited us apostles as last of all, as though sentenced to death, because we have become a spectacle to the world, to angels and to mortals. We are fools for the sake of Christ, but you are wise in Christ. We are weak, but you are strong. You are held in honor, but we in disrepute. To the present hour we are hungry and thirsty, we are poorly clothed and beaten and homeless, and we grow weary from the work of our own hands. When reviled, we bless; when persecuted, we endure; when slandered, we speak kindly. We have become like the rubbish of the world, the dregs of all things, to this very day.

Meditation

It is required of stewards that they should be found trustworthy. And what does trustworthy look like in our day and age? Is it enough to long for better things? Or must our longing and our grief at what is being lost eventually translate into action? When reviled, we bless; when persecuted, we endure; when slandered, we speak kindly. Is this what it means to be a good steward? To choose the better way for our lives and for our world?

The human story is over and over again a story of longing for better things not just for ourselves but even more ardently for our children. There is a depth of hopefulness and heroism that parents can access beyond the reach of mere mortals. It causes a mother to throw herself over her children to protect them from a shooter. It causes an old man to put himself in harm's way to defend a neighbor child from a gang of bullies. It compels an older sibling to risk drowning to rescue a little sister. This kind of deeply valiant heroism is found in those who are trustworthy. It's what we hope can be found in each of us, calling us forward into our most noble, hopeful, and undauntable selves.

Prayer

Faithful God, you dare us to trust in your benevolence. Faithful God, you invite us to live as you live, to act as you act, to remain faithful and trustworthy as you are. Faithful God, form us, mold us, shape us to be faithful and trustworthy actors in these perilous days.

Boy Begotten

Boy begotten, not made,
of one being with
   everything.
Boy awake on a hard bed, on fire
in the middle of the night,
   the terrible wail that woke him
   still echoing off into the silence.

I am burning; you will cool me.
I am untaught; you will tell me
             the secrets of the universe.
I am light only because of your Light,
      god only because you are God.

But are you prepared to know?
Torn away from the mouth of life, the long kiss of
             family, playmates, a lover?
Infused with Light . . .
are you prepared to become sacrament?

Thursday

1 Peter 4:1–2, 7–11

Since therefore Christ suffered in the flesh, arm yourselves also with the same intention (for whoever has suffered in the flesh has finished with sin), so as to live for the rest of your earthly life no longer by human desires but by the will of God.

The end of all things is near; therefore be serious and discipline yourselves for the sake of your prayers. Above all, maintain constant love for one another, for love covers a multitude of sins. Be hospitable to one another without complaining. Like good stewards of the manifold grace of God, serve one another with whatever gift each of you has received. Whoever speaks must do so as one speaking the very words of God; whoever serves must do so with the strength that God supplies, so that God may be glorified in all things through Jesus Christ. To God belong the glory and the power for ever and ever. Amen.

Meditation

It is a struggle to know how to respond to the needs of our world, of our suffering planet, and all those suffering as a result of the world's suffering. We are tempted to be over-whelmed, or acquiesce to what seems to be the inevitable, or simply to weep and rage at whatever forces thwart our best efforts to make change happen. I'm convinced that the key to not giving up is to "serve one another with whatever gift each of us has received." We are the body of Christ as surely as the earth is the body of the Trinity. When we work together, each tending our own small gardens, we create a space for heroism and miracles. We touch the porous edges of life's most rock-hard problems. Like sculptors carving from the edges to the center of a sculpture, our small chipping efforts given from our truest gifts combine with those of others to make the impossible possible. What we cannot see or even dare to dream today in our aloneness becomes our new vision shared together as we link hand in hand with the people of God. Take heart; take hands and share the gifts of your own hands to fashion a better tomorrow.

Prayer

You, the one who gives without end; you, the one who gifted us so that we might also give; you, the one who imagined into being a world where sharing sustains life: Show us our gifts so that we can learn how to offer them as a part of your great dream. If I can help, let me help. If I can create, let me create. If I can mend, let me mend. If I can build, let me build. If I can imagine, let me imagine alongside you. Together let us bring to the dream all that lies within us. Let us together become more than we have been, because in the sharing, in the dreaming, in the being our full selves within your beingness, we too become a force for holy life.

Morning Comes
(for a priest, longing)

Because you are a Creation of the Creator,
   you share ownership in holy dreams
   that give birth to new galaxies;
      you are fashioned in God's image—
      look at what the two of you have done together
              and be pleased!

Because you are sister to the prophets,
   you are no stranger to pain,
   or laughter, tears, anger or the hard things that must
      be said;
   you have helped us grow, marry and give birth;
   you have waited by our beds through sad nights
              and buried us.

Because you are the Hand of God,
   you make the sign of the cross in ashes and oil,
   you anoint, consecrate, baptize, bless and absolve;
      or in the secret solitude of your own room,
      do you sometimes simply pray, clinching your fists,
              for patience?

Because you are a Child of the Light,
   you are a fierce believer, and as in childbirth,
   purposeful in your labor;
      your work is sweaty, long, but joyful—
      you count a good day by the rising of the sun,
              as evening passes
              and morning comes.

Friday

Ephesians 4:1–16

I therefore, the prisoner in the Lord, beg you to lead
a life worthy of the calling to which you have been
called, with all humility and gentleness, with patience,
bearing with one another in love, making every effort
to maintain the unity of the Spirit in the bond of peace.
There is one body and one Spirit, just as you were
called to the one hope of your calling, one Lord, one
faith, one baptism, one God and Mother of all, who is
above all and through all and in all.

But each of us was given grace according to the
measure of Christ's gift. Therefore it is said,

"When he ascended on high he made captivity
itself a captive;
he gave gifts to his people."

(When it says, "He ascended," what does it mean but
that he had also descended into the lower parts of
the earth? He who descended is the same one who
ascended far above all the heavens, so that he might
fill all things.) The gifts he gave were that some would
be apostles, some prophets, some evangelists, some
pastors and teachers, to equip the saints for the work of
ministry, for building up the body of Christ, until all of
us come to the unity of the faith and of the knowledge
of the Son of God, to maturity, to the measure of the
full stature of Christ. We must no longer be children,

tossed to and fro and blown about by every wind of doctrine, by people's trickery, by their craftiness in deceitful scheming. But speaking the truth in love, we must grow up in every way into him who is the head, into Christ, from whom the whole body, joined and knitted together by every ligament with which it is equipped, as each part is working properly, promotes the body's growth in building itself up in love.

Meditation

"But speaking the truth in love, we must grow up in every way into the one who is the head, into Christ." The truths of our lives are not easy to speak. The truths of what the world is facing are not easy to hear. One way to respond to truth is to deny it. Plausible deniability is a regular practice of our sin-sick world. If only I can pretend I didn't know. If only I can refute the veracity of your argument. If only I can believe that my truth and your truth are not the same; and therefore we can never see eye to eye.

Christ said, "I am the Way, the Truth, and the Life." Can it be that even when there are many, many ways, there is a unity and coherency to those ways when lived in imitation of the life of Christ? Can it be that even as we all see truth from our own vantage point, there are truths too real for any of us to reject? And can it be that life as we know it, life lived in abundance, in diversity, teeming with new and wondrous possibilities, life lived for life, life lived in peace; life lived in hope; life lived in love of God and neighbor: can it be that such a life is a life that God dreams of for each of us?

We must no longer be children, naïve and unknowing. We must be the adult children of a God who dreamed the world into being and continues to cherish its goodness. See the goodness as God sees it. Be the goodness as Christ was and is. Live the goodness so that the children and grandchildren and great grandchildren who inherit this world from us know a world where none are despised, none are harassed, none are discounted, and none are forgotten. Live the life of the Christ in such a way that the world can see and know the beauty, the strength, and the power of God's divine goodness planted within us and the world around us.

Prayer

Mother Eagle, you kick us from the nest, not to leave you but in order for us to soar. The nest nurtures until the day we no longer fit within its confines. You made us to be eagles, not fledglings remaining children forever. We were conceived to swoop and rise and soar. Youth is a beautiful passageway, adolescence a door, but the highest heights lie waiting when we leave the safety of childhood and dare mount the winds and wing to unknown shores. Mother Eagle, the time has come for us to leave the safety of the nest, instead to dare to fly with you into heights of our best selves; the heights of truthfulness, the heights of courage, the heights of perceptiveness and wisdom. The time has come for us to build up your created body, the vast and complete cosmos, wide and deep fullness of life found in you. Mother Eagle, bless us in our flight.

The Un-Nesting

Afraid for your freefall,
I watch, helpless, as you plummet . . .
    but pure as birth,
    certain as the moment I first wanted you,
    I must be sure you will fly . . .
because it was me who pushed you from the nest.

What do you know of me?
What will you think of me
for sending you out this way?

I will feel my sadness apart from you.

But this is instinct.
This is the long labor,
my work to do here.

This is something inside of me,
knowing how to do
what I thought I could never do.

And will you prove me true?
Will you fall
       or un-nested, will you soar?

Saturday

1 Corinthians 13:1–13

If I speak in the tongues of mortals and of angels, but do not have love, I am a noisy gong or a clanging cymbal. And if I have prophetic powers, and understand all mysteries and all knowledge, and if I have all faith, so as to remove mountains, but do not have love, I am nothing. If I give away all my possessions, and if I hand over my body so that I may boast, but do not have love, I gain nothing.

Love is patient; love is kind; love is not envious or boastful or arrogant or rude. It does not insist on its own way; it is not irritable or resentful; it does not rejoice in wrongdoing, but rejoices in the truth. It bears all things, believes all things, hopes all things, endures all things.

Love never ends. But as for prophecies, they will come to an end; as for tongues, they will cease; as for knowledge, it will come to an end. For we know only in part, and we prophesy only in part; but when the complete comes, the partial will come to an end. When I was a child, I spoke like a child, I thought like a child, I reasoned like a child; when I became an adult, I put an end to childish ways. For now we see in a mirror, dimly, but then we will see face to face. Now I know only in part; then I will know fully, even as I have been fully known. And now faith, hope, and love abide, these three; and the greatest of these is love.

Meditation

For Paul, love was the key. So much so that it is near impossible to read the gospels without coming to this same conclusion. Love is the key. Love is, even in a world spinning into entropy where all matter and every carbon-based entity has a half-life, scripture tells us, still eternal. None of us can know what will become of our world as we know it. We have considerable scientific evidence to convince us that humans now have the capacity to destroy the cumulative work of God's good hands. But there is no evidence to support the notion that even if we do manage to destroy God's metaphorical hands, just as we managed to crucify the Christ, that God's hands can be destroyed.

The fear in saying this is always that the people of God can and will respond by taking a chair and waiting for God to fix what we have broken. If our world needs healing, we say, isn't it ultimately up to the great healer whether healing comes to that world? Aren't we too small, too powerless, too finite to fix what now seems near hopelessly broken?

And still we know that even our human love is eternal. Our love of man, woman, and child is eternal. Our love of river, mountain, and glade is eternal. Our love of dolphin, eel, and jellyfish is eternal. Our love of jasper, agate, and turquoise is eternal. Our love of crocus, primrose, and bear grass is eternal. We dare not quit loving all that God has made, because in the loving we touch the truest hands of God. We take part in the eternal. We create room for the eternal. We bind our destiny to the destiny of the stars, brimming with their matter and anti-matter. If ever there was a season for loving the world, we have entered it. If ever there was an earth-shattering necessity for love, we have come to that place of need.

Just as we crucified the Son of God and still love reigned, so we must let love reign in this day, in this time, in this way, in this truth, in this life, daring to hope and work and pray for something we cannot see. Daring to journey to the empty tomb with only love as our companion, longing, longing for better than what awaits us, longing for something eternal that can lift us to the thermals and leave us winged, untethered by our mortal pain and fear, and longing with our laboring world, longing for better things.

Prayer

O God of all that is and ever will be, teach us to long for better things.

Glacier Park, Montana

2017 WAS A HISTORIC SUMMER of fires in Glacier Park. It was also a historic summer of visitors. No national park had ever had a visitor count of one million visitors in one month before; this particular year saw three million visitors in one summer. Glacier Park offers clear evidence of the ways in which our natural world is changing. If you talk to someone who visited the park decades ago, their first question upon returning is where did all these people and cars come from? Their next question is what happened to the glaciers? The number of glaciers in the park has dramatically decreased since the middle of the nineteenth century. While it is difficult to get an exact count, it is likely that we've gone from 185 glaciers in the 1870s to eighty-five glaciers by the 1920s to perhaps twenty-five glaciers in 2017. Almost all the glaciers still intact have shrunk markedly (two have grown slightly as a result of their particular geography and geology) and with that shrinking comes changes in the entire ecosystem. But the shrinking of the glaciers is primarily one symptom of an even more impactful reality: climate change.

The fires of 2017 and 2018 may be a warning of what the new normal will look like with depleted small aquifers, lowered forest humidity coupled with substantial undergrowth, and ever-increasing risks of lost habitat from tree disease, worsened by rising temperatures. What is being created are new boundaries for habitat and with that come challenges for creatures that live at both ends of the mountains. The upper elevation creatures like picas have no space to escape to as their rocky barren environs gain new species of flora and fauna. Mountain goat habitat is also threatened. At the lower warmer ends of the mountainsides the risks of exotic invasions by foreign species are heightened with anticipated rising water and air temperatures.

While no one knows how long the glaciers will last, most predictions are that the majority of the surviving glaciers will be lost between 2020 and 2030 with perhaps one or two surviving in much smaller footprints. What this will mean for spring runoff and late summer water supplies is difficult to know yet. But every indication is that water issues will be critical not just to Glacier Park but also to the entire region fed from the aquifer below these mountains.

Water, that essential building block of all life. Water is sacred. Water is life. We affirm that so profoundly in our baptismal liturgies. The existing glaciers of Glacier Park are the last remains of ancient water, water that formed itself into glaciers at least seven thousand years ago and may have formed into ice as long ago as during the Pleistocene age. Geologists tell us there have been glaciers in this region of the earth for millions of years. If the earth is the body of God, then perhaps glaciers are God's priceless jewels, her royal diadem, her wedding garb. Like a bride adorned for her betrothed, God gives herself to us; in love, in fidelity, in trust. May we choose in this holy season to live as one worthy of her trust.

POSTSCRIPT

Now we have arrived at Holy Week, that most set apart of all times in our Christian lives. We, with Jesus, will turn our face toward Jerusalem; Jerusalem the symbol of our best and our worst, our hopes and our despairs. Our journey led us to this moment, a moment drenched in suffering and courage, hope, and escalating conflict. This holy week that stands before us is set apart from Lent in the Eastern tradition. It is ripe with its own focus and energy. In these most holy days we adjust our lives one more time and turn our gaze full on toward the mystery of God made flesh. God among us; a God who refused to give up on us even as we betrayed our own sacred callings. This week to come stands at the heart of the Christian year. We have prepared ourselves to be here, to see with new eyes, to embrace the gift of life with new fervor; and the church asks us to enter it with our whole selves. If we walk the Via Dolorosa, the way of suffering that leads to new life and new hope, if we journey with Christ—not just in the week to come but stepping forward into the breach from this moment on—then we reclaim God's dream for us and for our world. Christ's saving love becomes the source of our saving love. A love that has the power to govern and transform the world. Holy Week awaits us and invites us all to trust and leap.

Leap
An Easter Meditation

There is the quantum leap—the mostly theoretical ability to go great distances instantaneously by pleating the fabric of time; there is the leap of faith—the courage to step outside known boundaries, placing trust in the unseen; and there is leaping for joy—done most often by new lambs, healed cripples and children.

"Leap!" he commands, awakened and
   spirit only, from the edge of silent space
   and folded time.

> *It is in the new first hour, it is in new Light*
> *that, bewildered, we encounter God's perfect*
>   *improbability.*
> *I imagine you free of gravity and hurting flesh,*
> *complete in the company of angels*
>   *and a once-dead thief.*

"Leap," he then entreats gently,
   shaken and tired, man again at the unhinged stone
   of his own tomb.

This is an unreasonable morning,
   no science, no trickery can explain it.
     I wonder if, in your all-too-human need to find
     someone able to understand, you cry out:
        "Lazarus!"

"Leap!" he answers softly, close beside me.
    "Shut your eyes and leap, as if resurrection itself
    depends entirely upon it!"

> *My fragile trust,*
> *invited into the dim unknown;*
> > *fragile faith granted irrational Easter courage—*

Leap! and it shall be given to you like a gift.
Leap! and you shall find what you are longing for.
Leap! and even these mysterious Easter doors shall
        finally be thrown open.